BrightRED Results

LEARN TO LEARN

for Curriculum for Excellence

Shona Cochrane

First published in 2015 by:
Bright Red Publishing Ltd
1 Torphichen Street
Edinburgh
EH3 8HX

A CIP record for this book is available from the British Library

ISBN 978-1-906736-68-2

With thanks to:
PDQ Digital Media Solutions Ltd (layout), Sue Moody, Bright Writing Ltd. (edit)

Cover design and series book design by Caleb Rutherford – e i d e t i c

Acknowledgements
Every effort has been made to seek all copyright holders. If any have been overlooked, then Bright Red Publishing will be delighted to make the necessary arrangements.

Permission has been sought from all relevant copyright holders and Bright Red Publishing is grateful for the use of the following:

FrankRamspott/iStock.com (p 5); FrankRamspott/iStock.com (p 12); Helga Esteb/ Shutterstock.com (p 13); F. Schmutzer (public domain) (p 13); FrankRamspott/iStock.com (p 15); Helga Esteb/Shutterstock.com (p 16); FrankRamspott/iStock.com (p 17); FrankRamspott/ iStock.com (p 19); FrankRamspott/iStock.com (p 25); m-gucci/iStock.com (p 27); koya79/ iStock.com (p 28); FrankRamspott/iStock.com (p 29); BartekSzewczyk/iStock.com (p 30); FrankRamspott/iStock.com (p 31); ConstantinosZ/iStock.com (p 33); Caleb Rutherford e i d e t i c (pp 34 & 46); Africa Studio/Shutterstock.com (p 38); Tdadamemd (CC BY-SA 3.0)1 (p 41); FrankRamspott/iStock.com (p 45); FrankRamspott/iStock.com (p 47); FrankRamspott/ iStock.com (p 48); FrankRamspott/iStock.com (p 49); Caleb Rutherford e i d e t i c (p 49); FrankRamspott/iStock.com (p 50); Alexandre Duret-Lutz (CC BY-SA 2.0)2 (p 52); Zsuzsa N.K./freeimages.com (p 53); monkeybusinessimages/iStock.com (p 55); FrankRamspott/ iStock.com (p 55); Miguel Saavedra/freeimages.com (p 56); Generacionx/istockphoto (p 60); FrankRamspott/iStock.com (p 61); FrankRamspott/iStock.com (p 63); Marko Skrbic/ istockphoto (p 63); Mega Pixel/Shutterstock.com (p 64); jorge vicente/freeimages.com (p 65); Nomadic Lass (CC BY-SA 2.0)2 (p 66); Sergey Nivens/iStock.com (p 67); Tifonimages/ Dreamstime.com (p 68); algiamil/freeimages.com (p 69); shho/freeimages.com (p 73); FrankRamspott/iStock.com (p 75); Andreas Krappweis /freeimages.com (p 76); shironosov/ iStock.com (p 78); Caleb Rutherford e i d e t i c/iStock.com (p 79); ksyproduktor/iStock. com (p 81); FrankRamspott/iStock.com (p 81); FrankRamspott/iStock.com (p 83); alexandre saes/freeimages.com (p 83); FrankRamspott/iStock.com (p 85); robin_24 (CC BY 2.0)3 (p 91); wwarby (CC BY 2.0)3 (p 91); -=Vo=-/Shutterstock.com (p 91); Rashevskyi Viacheslav/ Shutterstock.com (p 91); robin_24 (CC BY 2.0)3 (p 92); Andres Rueda (CC BY 2.0)3 (p 92); Ruslan Ivantsov/Shutterstock.com (p 92); -=Vo=-/Shutterstock.com (p 92); LGEPR (CC BY 2.0)3 (pp 91 & 92); RTimages/Shutterstock.com (pp 91 & 92); Coprid/Shutterstock.com (pp 91 & 92); Kostyantyn Ivanyshen/Shutterstock.com (pp 91 & 92); Stankevich/Shutterstock.com (pp 91 & 92); NakarinZ/Shutterstock.com (pp 91 & 92); Voronin76/Shutterstock.com (pp 91 & 92); sh0dan (CC BY 2.0)3 (pp 91 & 92); Jebulon (public domain) (pp 91 & 92); Dobromila (CC BY-SA 3.0)1 (pp 91 & 92); Dakota Jackson Inc. (CC BY-SA 3.0)1 (pp 91 & 92); Questions from past exam papers © SQA (n.b. solutions do not emanate from the SQA) (pp 57, 58, 60, 71, 74, 78, 79).

(CC BY-SA 3.0)1   http://creativecommons.org/licenses/by-sa/3.0/
(CC BY-SA 2.0)2   https://creativecommons.org/licenses/by-sa/2.0/
(CC BY 2.0)3   http://creativecommons.org/licenses/by/2.0/

Printed and bound in the UK by Martins the Printers.

CONTENTS

INTRODUCTION

Aim of this study guide 4

1. LEARNING FOR LIFE

Learning as a process 6
The cycle of learning 8
The 3Rs: review, remember and recall 10

2. LEARNING AND THINKING STYLES

Learning about your strengths and weaknesses . . 12
Types of learner and thinker 14
What kind of thinker and learner are you? 16
How can you learn better? 18
Investigating learning styles 1 20
Investigating learning styles 2 22

3. WHAT STUDY SKILLS AND TECHNIQUES SHOULD YOU USE?

Using the 3Rs 1 24
Using the 3Rs 2 26
The 3Rs in practice – the ideal study hour 1 28
The 3Rs in practice – the ideal study hour 2 30
Study plan 32
Setting realistic goals and targets 34

4. REVIEW

Making notes – keywords 1 36
Making notes – keywords 2 38
Making notes – using prompts 1 40
Making notes – using prompts 2 42
Making notes – using prompts 3 44
Using and practising study skills 46

5. REMEMBER

Planning your study programme 48
Techniques for reinforcing and remembering information 1 50
Techniques for reinforcing and remembering information 2 52
Look/cover/write/check 54

6. RECALL

Techniques for recalling what you have learned 1 . . 56
Techniques for recalling what you have learned 2 . . 58
Techniques for recalling what you have learned 3 . . 60
Applying what you have learned 62
Planning essays and extended answers 64
Research 66
How to use quotes, references and avoid plagiarism 68
Self-assessment and correcting work 70

7. ASSESSMENT TECHNIQUES

Getting ready for exams 72
Before the exam 1 74
Before the exam 2 76
Before the exam 3 78
Before the exam 4 80
Answer plans 1 82
Answer plans 2 84
In the exam 86

8. EMPLOYABILITY AND ENTERPRISE SKILLS

Developing lifelong skills 88

9. APPENDICES

Appendix 1 – Instructions 90
Appendix 2 – Curriculum for Excellence: the four capacities 94

10. GLOSSARY   96

AIM OF THIS STUDY GUIDE

If you're reading this guide, you're probably preparing for SQA assignments and exams in National 4, National 5, Higher or Advanced Higher. The aim of the guide is to help you learn how to learn – to find out which style of thinking and learning works best for you – so you feel comfortable and motivated when you are studying for these qualifications. It also aims to help you develop study skills and techniques that you can use not only in school, but as part of your **lifelong learning**.

And don't forget that parents, family and friends can be a huge support to you during the study process – this guide shows them how.

THINKING AND LEARNING STYLES

Every learner is unique in the ways that they take in information, process it and retain it – in other words, how they think and learn. There are several **thinking and learning styles**. The key ones are:

- auditory
- visual
- kinaesthetic

You'll find out more about these in the 'Learning and thinking styles' chapter. Most of us are stronger in one or two styles, but it's important that you recognise which ones you are weaker in. By spending time learning and practising new study techniques, you will find that you can learn and recall much more information.

REFLECTIVE THINKING

You will find **reflective thinking** mentioned throughout this guide. It is a simple process that helps our brain to remember and apply information. With reflective thinking, you use **keywords** that act as prompts to link your memory to banks of information. You can then apply this information to a range of familiar and new contexts.

The reflective thinking process promotes the use of more **complex thinking skills** such as applying, analysing, evaluating and creating as outlined in Bloom's taxonomy (Anderson and Krathwohl, 2001). As you progress through school, the work becomes more complex, and you'll need these skills to complete more challenging assignments.

THE 3RS PROCESS – REVIEW/REMEMBER/RECALL

The review/remember/recall process is key to studying successfully for exams and assessments. It is described in detail throughout this guide. The **3Rs** process involves:

- gathering the information you want to learn
- retaining the information
- being able to recall and use the information when you need it in exams.

By using the 3Rs, you will learn and practise new study techniques, which in turn will enable you to learn what you need to know for your exams. Learning to use different techniques will ensure that you are able to use the best method for learning a particular piece of work, and will also keep your brain more alert, so you are less likely to get bored.

You can think about the 3Rs as a **learning cycle**.

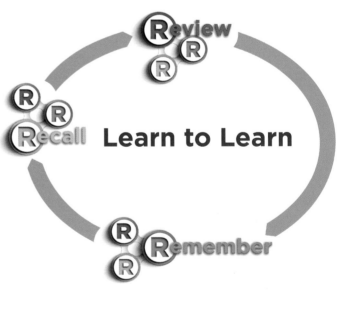

ACTIVE LEARNING AND STUDY

Active learning can mean different things to different people. For example, some people think that if they read over their work again and again, it will become more familiar and they will remember it. This isn't active learning.

Active learning and study uses a much higher degree of mental (and sometimes physical) involvement, by actually doing things with the information you are trying to learn.

> 'Active learning is learning which engages and challenges children's thinking using real-life and imaginary situations. All areas of the curriculum can be enriched and developed through active learning.'
>
> Education Scotland (2010)

As you become **active** in your learning and study, the amount and quality of what you learn improves. Active study is a part of each of the 3Rs stages. For example, in the remember stage, active study involves using various techniques to check if you can remember what you are trying to learn. You can do this on your own but your parents, family and friends can be a huge help too. You will learn more about this process as you work your way through this book.

WHAT IS STUDY?

Study involves using a variety of skills and techniques to help you to learn and prepare for exams and assignments.

All SQA assessments and exams cover a broad range of knowledge, understanding and skills. You will need to develop different study skills and techniques to handle these.

Once you have worked through this guide, you should develop a **study plan** that takes into account how you think and learn, the types of assessment and exams you are preparing for and the skills and techniques you will need to prepare for them. Your study plan should be developed and reviewed frequently.

THINGS TO DO AND THINK ABOUT

Involving your helpers

Getting other people to help with your study can be a real asset. The two main groups who can support your learning are your parents, guardians and family, and your friends or study buddies. There are lots of things they can help you with. For example, they can help you identify the bits you know well and the parts that need more work. These checking sessions can be fun, can take the loneliness out of learning and can make it more interesting. However, your helpers can get involved in other ways too.

LEARNING AS A PROCESS

This chapter will explore the basic study process. Study is a process that helps us to learn new and sometimes challenging material. It can develop our understanding and improve our ability to remember things – especially for important assessments, including exams. Success in formal assessments is often a key requirement for jobs or further courses, so it is important to know how to learn the ideas and concepts, and how to set out answers to score marks.

WE LEARN IN DIFFERENT WAYS

Your brain continues to learn as you grow. What you learn at school is only the start of your lifelong learning, and learning and **study skills** give you the ability to develop your learning processes and to adapt to a changing, developing society.

A few people are lucky enough to remember a lot of what they hear, or read, or see, but most people need to use a range of different methods to help the recall process. We are all unique and we learn and remember in different ways. **Study notes** and revision plans can be a great help – if we know how to use them. A successful **study programme** takes note of how an individual thinks and learns, then develops and practises a range of techniques that work for them.

LEARNING FOR CURRICULUM FOR EXCELLENCE

As you move through secondary school, assessments become increasingly formal to prepare you for the National 4 and 5, Higher and Advanced Higher exams you will sit in the senior years. **Curriculum for Excellence** covers a wide range of learning outcomes and uses different forms of assessment, so you have to prepare yourself by developing a wide range of study skills.

Working through this guide will help you to develop and improve your study and lifelong skills to become a **successful learner**, **confident individual**, **responsible citizen** and **effective contributor**. You will also learn **self-evaluation** and **reflective thinking** techniques which will help to improve your performance in all of your SQA assessments.

RED ARROW LEARNING TRIANGLE

As a learner, you have to be involved in your own education or it's a one-way process like the one illustrated below where the teacher is just **instructing** you, and you are not making the knowledge your own.

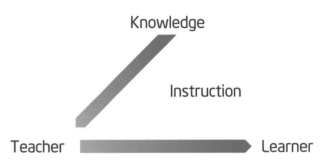

Education occurs when you, as the learner, are fully involved. The teacher selects interesting and exciting ways to present course materials and they inspire you to want to know more. You interact with your teacher by asking questions, giving suggestions and seeking to gain more knowledge.

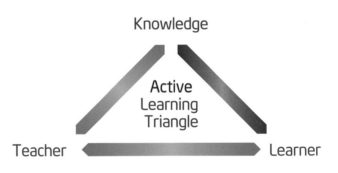

This red arrow stage is when the lasting brain connections are made. This is where you, as the learner, take ownership of the knowledge, making it **your** knowledge. Reflective thinking is a key part of the 'red arrow' process.

LIFELONG SKILL

This process – the red arrow learning triangle – will be important throughout your life as you develop your work skills to meet the demands of evolving careers. The teacher will be replaced by work colleagues or people who support work-based learning, but it is the red arrow stage that will help to ensure that you have the skills to be comfortable and able to do your job as it changes with time.

Some of you might even be doing jobs that haven't been thought about or created yet!

HOW DO I LEARN FOR EXAMS?

Learning is about thoroughly understanding **key concepts** and being able to convert that understanding into the acceptable responses required in written examinations and assignments.

Learning and studying can be a very rewarding – but also a very stressful – process. To maximise learning and minimise stress, you need to bring the components in the diagram to the right together in an organised study programme.

As well as helping you pass assignments and exams, effective study can be a major contributor towards your **health and wellbeing**.

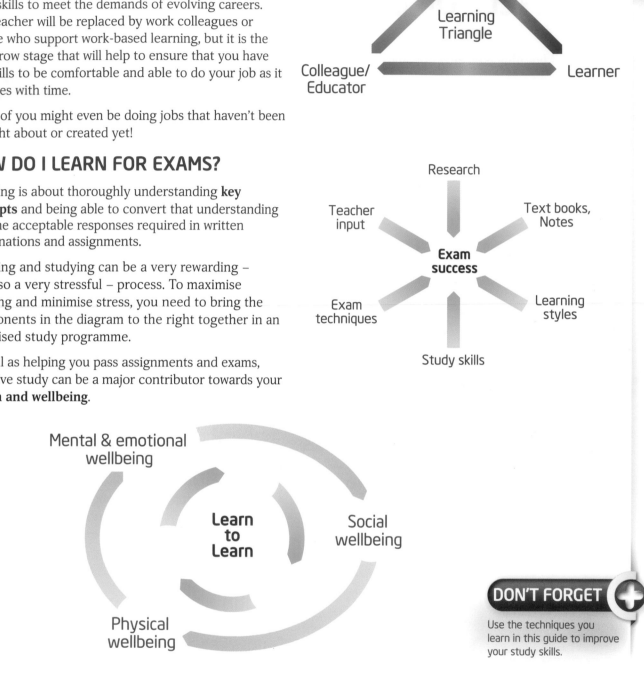

DON'T FORGET

Use the techniques you learn in this guide to improve your study skills.

THINGS TO DO AND THINK ABOUT

Success is usually measured publically by the results in exams, continuous assessments, project work and practical work. However, success is also a private thing. It is when you make progress and this includes the light bulb moments when everything suddenly falls into place, as well as the smaller achievements such as getting into a study routine or remembering a quote. Being aware of your achievements, big and small, helps to keep you motivated and keen to learn more.

Having confidence in your learning, and knowing that you have learned the work before you go into exams can help you to achieve mental and emotional wellbeing. Being organised will allow you to study and still leave enough time for your social activities, hobbies and your family. This, in turn, can help you feel energised, ready to study and able to meet all the other physical demands you encounter on a daily basis.

THE CYCLE OF LEARNING

The **cycle of learning** is an effective study process that leads to:

- successful learners
- effective contributors
- confident individuals

We're going to look at each part of the cycle in more detail.

CURRENT LEARNING HABITS

When you are developing your cycle of learning, look at your current learning habits and think about whether it might be productive to change some of them.

Your current learning habits include the ways that you use:

- homework
- study programmes
- study skills
- test and exam results
- previous experience.

① Current learning habits

② Identify thinking and learning styles

③ Organising your study

Review — Making notes

Remember — Study skills

Recall — Exam preparation

ACTIVITY:

	Think of a previous success in your favourite subject and try to answer truthfully how well you did with each of the following:	Very good	OK	Poor	Didn't do
1	Regularly spent time on homework				
2	Always studied before a test				
3	Revised the work regularly throughout the course				
4	Made study notes from books, handouts, etc.				
5	Used diagrams and/or mind maps				
6	Learned lists and was able to recite them				
7	Tested how well I remembered the key facts				
8	Always laid work out neatly and in an ordered way				
9	Made notes of areas which lost marks in tests				
10	Studied the areas where marks were lost in tests				

Now try this again for your least favourite subject. Are there key differences between the way you look at your favourite subject and least favourite subject? For example, do you spend as much time on your favourite subject as you do on your least favourite subject?

TOP TIP

Keep reading for practical advice on how to plan your study and take advantage of your individual **strengths** and build up your **weaknesses**.

IDENTIFY THINKING AND LEARNING STYLES

We all aim to get the best possible grades in our exams. However, we don't all learn and use the information in the same way. There are many styles of thinking – for example, in pictures, words or sounds, or by mentally or physically doing and practising something.

Different **thinking styles** work differently for different people, but knowing how best to use them can give you confidence when you are trying to learn.

For example, you might see someone listening carefully in class and know that they do relatively little study at home – yet they always do well in their tests. That could well make you feel inadequate. But don't let it! That student is probably an **auditory learner** who learns through hearing the sounds, and their way of studying and committing facts to their **long-term memory** is simply to recall in their own mind what was said during the lesson.

If you devise a study plan that plays to **your learning style**, then you will be able to recall the information just as well as the other student.

Developing an Active Study Plan

Once you've identified how you think, you can use this knowledge to build your auditory, visual and kinaesthetic preferences into an active study plan, where you get really involved with the information and start to think about it in new and challenging ways. This is active learning, and a key part of active learning is **reflective thinking**, which we touched on in the previous section.

Reflective Thinking

Reflective thinking is the process whereby you evaluate what you have covered in class (when you use your working memory) and start to store the information in your short- then long-term memory. This is an active thinking/study process. It helps your brain to internalise or make the information your own, so that you can recall it without prompts from your teacher or your notes.

Having this information stored in your short- and long-term memory allows your brain to apply this information to a wide range of contexts.

Reflective thinking is a **lifelong skill**. This means that you can use this process not just at school but throughout your working career to help you remember and process information.

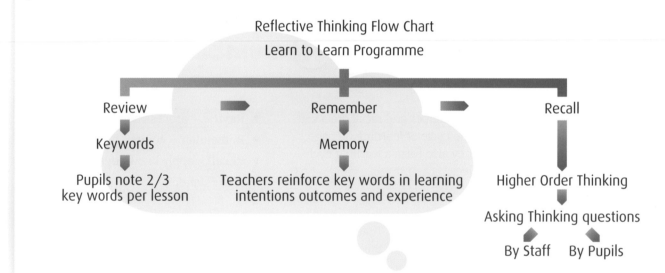

Reflective Thinking Flow Chart

Learn to Learn Programme

Review → Remember → Recall

Keywords — Memory

Pupils note 2/3 key words per lesson — Teachers reinforce key words in learning intentions outcomes and experience — Higher Order Thinking

Asking Thinking questions

By Staff By Pupils

ORGANISE YOUR STUDY

When you are working out how to organise your studying, you need to think about where and when you're going to study, the environment in which you're going to study (for example, music or no music?), and when you're going to take a break from studying.

Overall, your homework and study plan should be flexible enough to meet your learning needs and allow for your social time.

THE 3RS

In the next section, we're going to look at the other key stages of the cycle of learning – review, remember and recall. These are known as the '3Rs'. You'll remember that we also touched on these in the previous section.

DON'T FORGET

Make learning easier for your brain – **use** your preferred thinking and learning styles.

THINGS TO DO AND THINK ABOUT

Try to organise your study to suit what you are doing. For example – when can you listen to fast, lively music and when do you need silence?

THE 3RS: REVIEW, REMEMBER AND RECALL

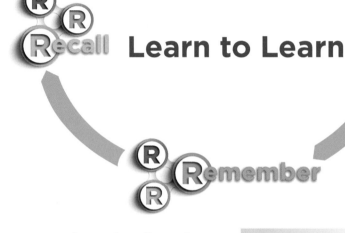

Learn to Learn

Review, remember and recall are a key part of the cycle of learning on page 8, and they also form a learning cycle themselves.

- **Review** – process new information
- **Remember** – commit to memory
- **Recall** – apply knowledge and understanding

REVIEW

Book Information

The **review** element of the 3Rs is perhaps the hardest and most crucial part of effective study. In this process, large quantities of information are broken down by identifying **keywords** or by using **diagrams** or other **visual cues** to **summarise** information. These keywords or visual cues then become **memory prompts**. The brain uses these prompts to recreate the more in-depth, detailed information required in assignments and exams.

You can make learning more interesting by turning these memory prompts into **rhymes**, **mnemonics**, diagrams and other cues. To do this effectively, you need to experiment with and practise study techniques so you can choose the ones that best suit your style of learning and the information that you want to learn.

REMEMBER

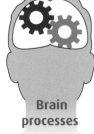

Brain processes

The **remember** part of the process commits information to the short- and long-term memory. Here, you use the memory prompts you developed in the review part of the process to help your brain to recall keywords and concepts, and expand them into the information required for answers.

To do this successfully, you have to **revisit** (go back to) work at **regular intervals**. For example, after your first learning session, you might revisit the work the next day, then one week later and then one month later. This not only helps with understanding but also commits the information to the long-term memory.

Having this information in your brain helps with assignments because you can add more depth and detail to your answers, and can apply your learning in more complex situations. It also allows you to cram more information into your **short-term memory** just before a test or exam.

RECALL

Knowing the material is not enough – you also need to be able to display your knowledge and skills in your exams and assessments. This is the **recall** stage of learning, where you have to use more complex thinking skills to apply your learning within a range of contexts. These thinking skills are outlined in the Bloom's *Taxonomy* six-stage thinking process:

Recall details

Higher Order Thinking Skills

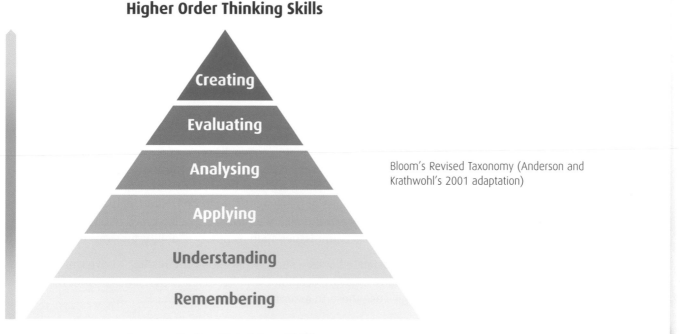

Creating

Evaluating

Analysing

Applying

Understanding

Remembering

Bloom's Revised Taxonomy (Anderson and Krathwohl's 2001 adaptation)

Lower Order Thinking Skills

The ability to understand, apply, analyse, evaluate and create can be learned, applied to each subject and practised to improve confidence in your learning and your grades.

The key instruction words used in assignments and exams – for example, describe, explain, and discuss – help you to **understand** and **interpret** what the examiners are looking for in your response. From this, you will be able to use the **higher order thinking skills** to adapt and apply the key information and specific **vocabulary** you have remembered to give a full answer to the question.

Evaluating your own strengths and weaknesses can significantly improve your exam performance. When a piece of marked work is returned, don't just look at the mark then move onto the next piece of work – evaluate it, and then you'll get to know what you should include in your answers and how much you need to write to achieve all the marks being awarded.

DON'T FORGET ✚

The recall stage helps us to apply higher order thinking skills in our work.

DON'T FORGET ✚

Use all stages of the 3Rs – **review, remember** and **recall**.

THINGS TO DO AND THINK ABOUT

Always spend some time looking over your marked work to see where you gained and where you missed out on marks.

LEARNING ABOUT YOUR STRENGTHS AND WEAKNESSES

This chapter will help you to investigate and identify how **you** think and learn, and this involves identifying your strengths and weaknesses.

Everyone has strengths in some areas of learning and weaknesses in others. If you know and understand your areas of strength, you can play to them. If you know and understand your areas of weakness, you can use techniques to improve them.

When people talk about thinking and learning, they tend to talk about intelligence, or being clever, in the same breath. But what does being clever mean?

WHAT IS INTELLIGENCE?

Many people have tried to define intelligence. IQ tests were pioneered by the French psychologist Alfred Binet in the early years of the twentieth century as a way of measuring intelligence. The tests have been refined over time, but critics have warned that the results of these tests should be treated with caution, because they are a measure of the ability to answer specific types of questions and don't take into account issues such as practical ability, motivation and anxiety.

More sophisticated tests – such as psychometric testing – have since been developed to measure academic intelligence and personality traits. Some companies use these to assess prospective employees.

Towards the end of the twentieth century, the American psychologist Howard Gardner introduced the theory of multiple intelligences. He developed the idea of seven basic intelligences:

- linguistic (language)
- logical–mathematical
- bodily–kinaesthetic (art)
- musical (rhythmic)
- spatial (physical)
- interpersonal (understanding other people)
- intrapersonal (understanding self)

Generally, people are strongest in one or two areas and can be quite weak in other areas. For example, somebody might have good linguistic ability and be good at learning new languages, but have poor spatial intelligence and not be good at physical activities.

This can result in learners really enjoying some subjects but feeling uncomfortable and lacking in confidence with others. It is important to appreciate that it is normal to be better at one or two of Gardner's types of intelligence. This can help to explain why some things seem easier than others.

ACTIVITY

Which of these areas are you strongest in?
Do these strengths tie into your strongest subjects?

WHO IS THE GENIUS?

Who would you say was a genius – Albert Einstein, an outstanding physicist, or David Beckham, an outstanding footballer? Here are some of their achievements to help you make up your mind.

Albert Einstein

Born 14/03/1879 – died 18/04/1955

Physicist.

Awarded the Nobel Prize for Physics in 1921.

Achievements included:
general and special relativity theories; Brownian motion; photoelectric effect; mass-energy equivalence ($E = mc^2$); Einstein field equations; unified field theory; Bose–Einstein statistics; EPR paradox.

David Beckham

Born 02/05/1975

Footballer.

Awarded the OBE in 2003.

Achievements include:
15 caps for England; captained England 2000–2006; highest paid footballer in the world in 2013; first British player to win league titles in four countries (England, Spain, the United States and France); appeared in three FIFA World Cups; six English Premier League titles; two FA Cup medals; UEFA Champions League in 1999; first British player to play 100 Champions League matches; UEFA Club Player of the year 1999; UNICEF Goodwill Ambassador 2006.

Under the traditional IQ categories, Einstein would be the obvious choice. However, if we use Gardner's multiple intelligence theory, then Einstein would be a genius in the logical–mathematical intelligence area while Beckham would be a genius in the spatial intelligence area.

Although we can't all be an Einstein or a Beckham, we can try to maximise the qualities we have to help us achieve our best. This will be easiest in our strongest subjects, but if we are weaker in one of the core subjects such as English or maths, then there are tips we can use to help us learn, understand and remember information that doesn't sit happily within our thinking and learning styles.

DON'T FORGET

It's natural to have stronger and weaker areas.

THINGS TO DO AND THINK ABOUT

Did you know that your areas of strength could lead you into a career that you haven't thought about yet? Investigate possible career pathways on the Skills Development Scotland website (www.myworldofwork.co.uk).

TYPES OF LEARNER AND THINKER

RIGHT-BRAIN AND LEFT-BRAIN LEARNERS

The brain is made up of two halves or hemispheres, which are simply called **the right brain and the left brain**. Each half is responsible for different ways of thinking.

Most people tend to be dominant in one particular hemisphere, although some people use both hemispheres almost equally. How we use our hemispheres affects how we evaluate issues and make decisions. For example, the right brain will look at the whole picture while the left brain will split this into smaller, more sequential steps.

This table shows some of the processes of each hemisphere.

Left brain	Right brain
Remembers words, vocabulary	Remembers images, pictures, shapes
Remembers names	Remembers faces
Works through things step-by-step	Considers a range of things simultaneously
Is a good timekeeper	Finds time seems to run out
Is organised	Is disorganised
Reads instructions at the start	Reads instructions as they do it
Listens to what is said	Listens to how it is said
Is objective, looks for facts	Is subjective, looks for trends

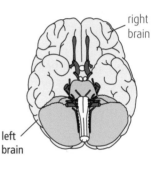

right brain

left brain

The curriculum in school generally favours left-brain activities, although activities such as role play, adding movement to reading and using colourful mnemonics are sometimes used in the classroom and would, for example, help right-brained pupils to learn a text.

Right-brain activity absorbs large bits of information but it needs the left-brain activity to sift through the information and organise it into an order so it can be used effectively. Study skills try to encourage the brain to use both hemispheres.

ACTIVITY

Using the star rating below, mark the appropriate number of stars against each of the characteristics in the table above that apply to you:

★   applies occasionally

★★   applies sometimes

★★★ applies a lot

Look at the spread of stars. Do you have most of your stars on one side? This means that you are dominant in that hemisphere. If your stars are spread through both right and left, then you are more 'whole brained'.

THE BRAIN – MAKING CONNECTIONS

The brain is an amazing organ. It makes thousands of connections every second from the information it takes in through our five senses – sight, smell, touch, taste and sound – and then sifts through the information to make sense of it. The primary function of this is to keep us safe and secure, but the most astounding thing is that our brain does all of this without us even being aware of it!

There has been a lot of research into how the brain works, and there are still many unanswered questions. Nobel prize winner Daniel Kahneman noted that the brain has two systems: system 1, the subconscious part, and system 2, the conscious, controllable part.

System 1 takes all the information it receives and tries to link it to previous experience or knowledge. The more often these links are made, the better the brain is at using them, so repeating things helps us to learn as our brains can recall the information more readily. We can even get to the stage where the brain can retrieve information or perform an action without consciously thinking about it.

The control we have over system 2 lets us make decisions that can overrule the initial reactions of system 1. System 2 is heavily involved in making the connections necessary for the higher order thinking skills outlined in the revision of Bloom's *Taxonomy*. Again, the more often these connections are made, the easier it is for the brain to recall and apply them.

DON'T FORGET

The more you use and exercise your brain, the more efficient it becomes!

DON'T FORGET

We are all unique learners, so we have to find a range of techniques that work best for us.

AUDITORY, VISUAL AND KINAESTHETIC THINKING AND LEARNING

There are three main types of thinking that impact on how you learn:

- **auditory** – hearing the task
- **visual** – seeing the task
- **kinaesthetic** – doing the task

It is best if you can use skills from each of these categories.

Auditory Thinkers

Auditory thinkers tune in to what they hear. Their brains can make connections easily by listening to everything in the classroom. This can be the teacher explaining, class and group discussions, video materials or auditory IT. They tend to 'hear' words in their heads. They probably remember keywords or phrases or even remember particular sounds and associate them with certain banks of knowledge.

Auditory thinkers find it easier to learn from teachers who have interesting voices and in classes where there are a lot of verbal question-and-answer sessions and discussion. They probably find reciting information (either out loud or in their heads) a useful way to remember, particularly if they are using interesting rhymes and rhythms.

Visual Thinkers

For **visual thinkers**, it is what they see that helps their brains to make the connections. They will feel comfortable in classrooms which have interesting visual displays. Rooms with piles of books, jotters and lots of clutter can make them feel less relaxed because there is too much random stimulation to their visual senses.

Interesting visual displays will help visual thinkers' brains to make the connections they need to internalise their knowledge. Visual learners could find that they recall teacher demonstrations or remember images in their minds of the teacher talking, the layout of information on the board or the positions of headings, bullet points or diagrams in a book or jotter.

Kinaesthetic Thinkers

For **kinaesthetic thinkers**, it is all about doing – either **physically** doing something or **mentally** rehearsing it in their brain.

For example, physically doing something could include trying something out after a teacher or role model has demonstrated it. This could cover a whole range of activities – from the skills and techniques required in practical subjects such as PE, art, technology and science to working through examples in maths, English and science.

Mental rehearsal takes the brain through all the connections it would make for a physical activity, but just misses out the last part of physically doing it. Going over something again and again in their minds is a very effective way for kinaesthetic thinkers to remember and process information.

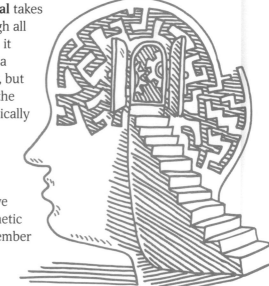

THINGS TO DO AND THINK ABOUT

As a learner, you are unique, and should investigate what works best for you. Use the activities on the next few pages to establish what type of thinker/learner you are. You can then use this information to improve on weak areas and play to your strengths when you are studying.

WHAT KIND OF THINKER AND LEARNER ARE YOU?

As you learned in the previous section, there are three main types of thinker – **auditory**, **visual** and **kinaesthetic**. Your thinking style links directly into your learning style so, for example, if you are an auditory thinker, your preferred learning style will be auditory.

Use the next activity to find out what your **preferred thinking and learning styles** are.

ACTIVITY

Try answering the following by circling A, B or C. This is just a bit of fun and will only give you a brief guide to your preferred style.

1 Your school is running its own X-Factor competition. You are discussing one of the acts with your friend. Do you:

    A remember the name of the act straight away?
    B see the person's face and the outfit they wore ?
    C talk about the dance routine they performed?

2 You are in your history class, studying the Romans. Would you prefer to:

    A listen to your teacher recount a famous battle?
    B watch a film of an exciting battle?
    C use your knowledge and play the part of a centurion in a battle re-enactment?

3 What type of text book would you prefer? One with:

    A loads of facts?
    B colourful illustrations?
    C lots of activities to do on your own or in groups?

4 You want to write down a word but you are not sure how to spell it. Do you:

    A sound the word out in your head, breaking it down into chunks?
    B see the different spellings and the shape of the word in your mind's eye?
    C write down the alternatives and choose which looks right?

5 You have been given the job of putting your group's work into a PowerPoint presentation. A computer specialist tells you exactly how to lay it out. Do you remember the instructions by:

    A recalling what you were told?
    B visualising how the presentation would look after each instruction?
    C working out which processes to do in order?

6 A tourist stops you and asks for directions to the swimming pool. Which of these descriptions would you be most likely to give?

    A Take the first left, travel for 200m, turn right and the pool is 100m on your right.
    B At that corner there, turn left. When you see the chip shop turn right and you'll see the pool on your right.
    C Go up to the corner and turn left. Carry on up the hill until you get to the chip shop then turn right. It's only a short distance along the road on your right.

Count up the number of times you circled A, B and C. Use the guide below to find your preferred thinking style and read the description of the one you had most of. Then read the others – are there things in there that are like you too?

DON'T FORGET

Remember, this is just a guide. An accurate analysis of your thinking style would need a lot more investigation.

If your answers were mainly:

A Your preferred thinking style is **auditory**. Do you enjoy listening to audio files, taking part in discussions, reading, language games and/or interviewing? You will probably remember telephone numbers by **chunking** the number into three groups, and reciting it in your head, getting a rhythm to the sounds.

B Your preferred thinking style is **visual**. You will probably enjoy using some or all of the following: graphs and charts, video presentations, the white board and interactive board or data projectors, classroom displays, colourful books and interesting pictures. You might see the pattern on the keypad that a phone number makes or you might visualise the number written down.

C Your preferred thinking style is **kinaesthetic**. This means that you remember better when you are physically doing things. You probably like role-play, field trips, making posters of key points, practical work, writing things out and/or making your own diagrams.

Which one is most like you? Most people will find that they are strongest in one, but sometimes like doing things from the others. It is best if you can use a wide range of methods to help you remember and recall. If you are really strong in one area, you might find it difficult to try out new study skills. Stick with it! It will be worth it in the end.

USING YOUR PREFERRED THINKING STYLES IN YOUR LEARNING

Since people think in different ways, it is important that their learning style incorporates and reflects their preferred thinking style. For example, if you are a visual thinker, it's important that your study notes are interesting and attractive so your eye will flow over the colours, patterns and shapes, and will help you take in the information.

THINGS TO DO AND THINK ABOUT

Don't just concentrate on your preferred thinking and learning styles – to study effectively, you'll need to get out of your comfort zone and practise new skills and techniques, such as learning lists of objects. This will also help to make your study more interesting and could help you to learn a wider range of material.

HOW CAN YOU LEARN BETTER?

In the last section, you learned about the type of thinker and learner you are. Now use that knowledge to help you to understand how you can learn better by going through the range of games and tasks over the next few pages. You will need to ask someone to help you with the games.

MEMORY GAMES

The following memory games will help you work out how you learn. The instructions and materials for the questions are in the Appendix at the back of the book (pages 90–94). Don't look at these materials before you start the games.

Expect to do better in some games and less well in others. Don't worry if you don't score as highly in a couple of games – they are used to work out your unique learning preferences and you will naturally be stronger in some than in others. Once you understand how you learn, you can develop different methods to help you to remember. This is really important to know as your study programme should certainly include the styles you are best at.

STUDY SUPPORT

You will need someone to help you with the games, so why not make it more fun by including your family or friends? Ask them to read the instructions on p90 and direct you in these games.

ACTIVITY

MEMORY GAME 1A – VISUAL

Look at the objects on Sheet A (page 91) for **one minute exactly**. Remember as many of the objects as you can. Do not look at the objects again. Do not write anything down until the end of the minute. At the end of the minute, write down as many of the objects as you can remember below:

_____   _____   _____

_____   _____   _____

_____   _____   _____

_____   _____   _____

Check your answers with your helper and total up your score out of 15.

ACTIVITY

MEMORY GAME 1B – VISUAL

Now look at the objects on Sheet B (page 92) for one minute exactly. Do not look at the objects again. Do not write anything down until the end of the minute. Your helper will ask you a question about the objects. Write your answers below:

_____   _____

_____   _____

Check your answers with your helper and total up your score out of 4.

You might have used some strategies to help you to remember the objects. Did you:

- remember the colours?   Yes/NO
- remember the positions on the page?   Yes/NO
- say or see the pictures or words in your mind's eye?   Yes/NO
- relate the items to real-life situations?   Yes/NO
- use something else?   Yes/NO

I found the thing that most helped me remember was _____

- Did you find seeing many of the same pictures in Sheet B confusing?   Yes/NO
- Did you realise quite quickly that some pictures were the same and
  some were different?   Yes/NO

I found the different pictures game easier/harder. (Underline your answer.)

DON'T FORGET

You will naturally be stronger in some of these games than in others. They are designed to establish what your areas of strength are.

THINGS TO DO AND THINK ABOUT

Every learner is a unique individual. If something in one of these games worked for you, make sure that you use it in your study programme.

INVESTIGATING LEARNING STYLES 1

STUDY SUPPORT

Your helper should read the instructions on p90 and direct you in these games.

ACTIVITY

MEMORY GAME 2A – AUDITORY

Your helper will read out a list of items from List 1 (page 93) **twice**. Try to remember as many items as you can. Do not look at the list or write anything down until the list has been read for the second time. Write your answers below:

_____ _____ _____

_____ _____ _____

_____ _____ _____

_____ _____ _____

_____ _____

Check your answers with your helper and total up your score out of 14.

MEMORY GAME 2B – AUDITORY

Repeat the process with the second list. Your helper will read out a list of items from List 2 (page 93) **twice**. Try to remember as many items as you can. Do not look at the list or write anything down until the list has been read for the second time. Write your answers below:

_____ _____ _____

_____ _____ _____

_____ _____ _____

_____ _____ _____

_____ _____

Check your answers with your helper and total up your score out of 14.

You might have used some strategies to help you remember the items. Did you:

- have any special strategies?   Yes/No
- realise the first list was alphabetic?   Yes/No
- say or see the words in your mind's eye?   Yes/No
- relate the items to real-life situations?   Yes/No
- use something else?   Yes/No

Was there anything that made it particularly difficult to remember some of the objects?

- Was there any item you didn't recognise?   Yes/No
- Were there too many items on the list?   Yes/No

The bit I found easiest was _____

The bit I found hardest was _____

Did you find it easier remembering words or pictures? (Underline your answer.)

I found words/pictures easier to remember.

DON'T FORGET

If you found games 2a and 2b trickier than games 1a and 1b, don't be disheartened. You might be more of a visual learner.

ACTIVITY

MEMORY GAME 3 – VISUAL

Your helper will show you a listing from a TV guide (page 93.). Look at the list for one minute exactly and try to remember as much as you can. Do not look at the list again. Do not write anything down until the end of the minute. Your helper will ask you some questions from the instructions. Write your answers below:

_____   _____   _____

_____   _____   _____

_____   _____   _____

_____   _____

Check your answers with your helper and total up your score out of 11.

What helped you to remember?

- Programmes you watch or know   Yes/No
- Informed guess   Yes/No
- Remembering character   Yes/No
- Visualising the programme   Yes/No
- Other prompts   Yes/No

Did you find the list of words easier to remember
than the pictures in game 1a and game 1b?   Yes/No

ACTIVITY

MEMORY GAME 4 – AUDITORY

Your helper will read you a list of football results (page 93) **twice**. Try to remember as many results as you can. Do not look at the list or write anything down until the list has been read for the second time. Your helper will ask you some questions from the instructions. Write your answers below:

1. _____   3. _____   5. _____

2. _____   4. _____   6. _____

Check your answers with your helper and total up your score out of 6.

- Did you find this easier or harder than the other memory games?   Yes/No
- Are you interested in football?   Yes/No
- Did you use strategies to remember?   Yes/No
- Did you guess some answers?   Yes/No

THINGS TO DO AND THINK ABOUT

When you are in class, the teacher will often talk to you about a new concept using pictures or diagrams or demonstrations. Do you find it easier to learn with a teacher rather than by reading things for yourself from a book? If so, could it be because they are tapping into more than one of your learning styles?

INVESTIGATING LEARNING STYLES 2

STUDY SUPPORT

Your helper should read the instructions on pxx and direct you in these games.

ACTIVITY

MEMORY GAME 5 – KINAESTHETIC

In this game you are going to try to remember how to spell some hard-to-learn words:

- onomatopoeia
- conscientious
- counterfeit
- beautiful
- necessary
- geography

1. Choose any two words from the list above that you find difficult to spell. (If you can already spell all these words, go to a dictionary and choose alternative words that you find hard to spell, or use a subject vocabulary list if you have one.) Write each word down ten times, trying to remember the order of the letters. Cover up your lists. Now write out the two words and check the spellings.

2. Choose two different words from the list (or select your own as above). Say them to yourself, either out loud or quietly in your head. Try to say them as they are written, not as they are properly pronounced. Repeat each word at least ten times. Cover up the words. Now write out the words and then check the spellings.

3. Use the last two words (or select your own as above). Try to split the word up into chunks that you can manage. For example, conscientious could become con scien (as in science) tious. Now learn the chunks using either or both of the methods above.

4. Which method was most effective for you?

   - Writing out the words   Yes/No
   - Saying them to yourself   Yes/No
   - Splitting the word   Yes/No

TOP TIP

If you found memory game 5 difficult, try using both methods – writing out and reciting (saying it over and over). Both auditory and visual learners can use this kind of repetition – it is not purely a kinaesthetic method.

DON'T FORGET

Repetition or practice is a vitally important part of the learning process for everyone – no matter what type of thinker or learner you are. Make sure you build it into your study programme.

HOW DO YOU LEARN BEST?

Having played the memory games how do you think you learn best? Do you prefer:

- listening and being told the information (games 2 and 4)?

  This is **auditory** learning.

- seeing the information (games 1 and 3)?

  This is **visual** learning.

- actually physically doing the tasks such as writing it down yourself (game 5)?

  This is **kinaesthetic** learning.

HOW DOES MY LEARNING STYLE AFFECT ME IN THE CLASSROOM?

Auditory Thinkers

Auditory thinkers often speak well in class discussions and do well with work that involves listening skills.

TOP TIP

Use keywords and subject-specific vocabulary in your reflective thinking, study and classwork.

They can seem much cleverer than you are. This is not necessarily the case. Everyone needs to use their own methods to learn information, so although visual and kinaesthetic thinkers might need to take more time to go through the learning process, it certainly doesn't mean that they are less able.

Auditory thinkers should try to identify the keywords and subject-specific vocabulary the teacher uses. They also need to learn a range of study skills. Often they can cope really well in the first few years at secondary school. However, as the work becomes more complex and they are required to do their own **research**, they will struggle if they do not have the range of skills that visual and kinaesthetic thinkers have practised for years.

Visual Thinkers

Strong **visual thinkers** will probably prefer lessons that use a lot of visual resources. They find it easier to remember material that is presented in diagrams, pictures or colour. They prefer colourful textbooks or **internet** resources to black-and-white handouts. Similarly, they can also find long blocks of text quite difficult to work through, because the layout is boring for their brains.

TOP TIP

Make mainly auditory lessons more interesting by creating colourful or well-laid-out notes with headings and subheadings for key points, and by highlighting subject-specific vocabulary.

Kinaesthetic Thinkers

Kinaesthetic thinkers often prefer practical sessions where they are able to physically move about. They learn best when they get a chance to practise the process the teacher has explained – for example, in maths, they will be comfortable working through various problems once the teacher has gone over an example. Some kinaesthetic thinkers find that doodling helps them to concentrate. If that's you, be careful not to become more interested in the doodle than the lesson!

Noting down the key points and subject-specific vocabulary during lessons will help kinaesthetic thinkers to remember them.

TOP TIP

Use highlighters and underlining to help you get active and engaged with the information in notes and handouts.

DON'T FORGET

Although you will naturally be stronger in some areas, try to use at least one technique from each thinking style.

EXTROVERTED AND INTROVERTED THINKING CONTINUUM

Your brain tends to make connections and develop ideas in one of two ways: **extroverted thinkers** prefer to talk and discuss to get their brain to understand and categorise information while **introverted thinkers** prefer to quietly work it through in their minds.

Extroverted/Introverted thinking continuum

Extrovert ⟵━━━━━━━━━━⟶ Introvert

develops ideas through: activity, discussion, interaction with others

develops ideas through: quiet concentration, reading, reflecting, working alone

Swiss psychiatrist Carl G Yung did a substantial study on extroverted and introverted thinkers. He found that extroverted thinkers tend to develop ideas through discussion. They like being in a classroom where there is lots of discussion, question and answer sessions and opportunities to interact with others to help develop and internalise new information.

By contrast, introverted thinkers like to be quiet and on their own while their brains make the internal connections. They often prefer to work privately through something rather than trying it out publicly. If you are an introverted thinker, you might feel uncomfortable when your teacher asks you a question while you are still processing the information. However, your teacher will only be doing this to try to assess your understanding and give you any support you need. Don't worry about being unsure of an answer – this is an important part of the learning process for both introverted and extroverted learners. If you never feel unsure about an answer or never get it wrong, then the work is too easy! You can learn a lot from a wrong answer.

As a learner, you will lie somewhere along the extrovert/introvert continuum. If you strongly prefer the characteristics of one, then you will be nearer that end of the continuum. If you use both equally, then you will be in the middle. This position could vary according to the task or subject.

THINGS TO DO AND THINK ABOUT

Think about your favourite class. Where do you lie along the extroverted/introverted thinking continuum for that class? Is it the same for your other classes?

USING THE 3RS 1

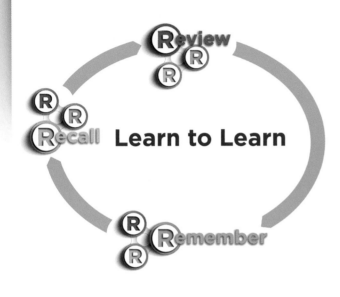

Learn to Learn

Now that you have identified your unique learning style preferences, let's get down to the nitty-gritty of learning about study techniques and how to use them to boost your study skills.

The next three chapters look at the study techniques for reviewing, remembering and recalling data – the 3Rs of study.

SOME FACTS ABOUT LEARNING

- 80–96 per cent of everything we learn is forgotten within 24 hours. Materials learned in class need to be looked at again later.
- It is as important to review as it is to learn something new. This helps to commit information to your memory.
- Reviewing is the difference between remembering and forgetting. Your study programme is vitally important.

You can address all of the above by using the simple three-stage study process – the 3Rs. It starts with you accessing information and ends with your successful performance in exams and assignments.

REVIEW

The review process has three essential stages:

- reflective thinking
- looking over classroom notes, books and homework
- making notes of key points.

Reflective Thinking

Reflective thinking involves spending a few minutes every evening thinking over what you did and identifying the keywords from each of your classes for that day. For some people, that will involve visualising or going through events, while for others it might be talking it through, either out loud or in their head. This starts to lodge more of the material in your memory.

By identifying the keywords, your brain will link them to information associated with them. For example, the keyword 'volcano' will trigger your brain to remember the shape of the volcano, eruptions and vents. By doing this, your brain starts to make its own connections between the keywords and the bank of associated information. These connections are specific to **your** brain – they are **your** connections. Once these connections are made, the information becomes **your** information and **your** learning.

Look Over

Like reflective thinking, looking over classroom notes, books and other teaching material should be done soon after the material is first introduced. This means that for homework or study, you should look over the work at least once per week for every subject. Looking at your notes and books adds to the reflective thinking process, because it covers some of the depth and detail that didn't readily come to your mind during reflective thinking. It helps to build and plug any gaps in your knowledge.

Helping your brain to make the connections between keywords and the related information makes it easier for it to recall and apply it.

Make Notes

When you have read over classroom materials, you should start to note keywords in ways that work best for you. These keywords will act as memory prompts. When your brain recognises the keywords its **system 1** (see page 14) will automatically search its memory banks for related information.

The keyword prompts can be written, but they can also take the form of **diagrams**, abbreviations and mnemonics. By using these techniques, you give the brain the information codes that it uses to make the connections. Your brain will be more stimulated if you use a range of techniques, because it will get bored and be less effective if you always use the same prompt – for example, mnemonics or bullet points.

Try saying out loud and recording the keywords, new vocabulary and drafts for oral assessments on the voice recorder of your mobile phone, or on your iPod or MP3 player. This can improve your confidence with spoken tasks.

DON'T FORGET

Your thinking style during the review stage can be auditory, visual or kinaesthetic – or a mixture of these styles.

THINGS TO DO AND THINK ABOUT

Try to get into the habit of making brief notes using **both** reflective thinking and your classroom notes.

USING THE 3RS 2

REMEMBER

Remembering is about committing information to your memory. It is about repeatedly making the connections in your brain until they become automatic when you use the key prompts. When you have practised making these connections enough, you will no longer need to be prompted by your teacher, books or notes to remember the information. This is when the information truly becomes **your** information and **your** learning!

Remembering is the process that takes the information in your **working memory** and helps you to store it in your short-term and then long-term memory.

To help store information, you can use active learning activities such as:

- repeating key words and phrases to make them more familiar
- checking how much you can understand and remember when looking over the notes you made during the review stage
- using keywords and prompts in your brief notes to trigger your brain to remember background information to rebuild the bigger picture, similar to the information in your textbook or class notes.

Working Memory

Your working memory is when your brain is dealing with new or challenging information. At this stage, connections are being made in the brain between new and existing information. For example, in second-year maths, you will get new information about algebra. Your brain will search for the information from first year and blend the experiences together to help you handle the more complex information.

Short-term Memory

In the classroom, experiencing information in a range of settings – such as teacher demonstration, group work or written exercises – uses a variety of thinking styles and helps to make the information more familiar, so it can be stored in the short-term memory.

Long-term Memory

By repeatedly making connections between keywords and related banks of information, you will help your brain to process these connections without thinking about it. This is when the long-term memory internalises the information and remembers for a long time.

If you look over your study notes over a period of time, this will help to keep them in your mind and commit information to your long-term memory. To do this, you need to look over your notes:

- after one week
- after one month
- after three months.

TOP TIP

Committing more information to your long-term memory over time will let you add extra things to your short-term memory just before tests.

RECALL

The recall process is the part of the 3Rs that is ultimately measured by success in assignments and exams. There are several ways that you can improve this. For example, you can practise techniques such as recognising key concepts and using the correct vocabulary to get more marks in assessments. Or you can simulate exam conditions using **past papers** and work to **exam timings** to develop your exam style and boost your confidence. This is another element of active study (see page 5).

TOP TIP

Try to structure your study to follow the 3Rs process for your favourite subject. Once you have achieved that, do the same for your other subjects.

DON'T FORGET

The 3Rs ▶ **Review** ▶ **Remember** ▶ **Recall** = **Active Study**

THINGS TO DO AND THINK ABOUT

Thinking skill acquisition

In 1967 two men called Fitts and Posner published their theory for learning and developing skills in sport. Their principles apply to the thinking process and help explain why the 3Rs are so effective.

There are three stages to learning and developing skills in sport:

- The **cognitive** stage – the new skill or information is introduced.
- The **associative** stage – there is a lot of repetition and practice.
- The **autonomous** stage – the skill becomes automatic and can be adapted to different contexts.

This ties into the 3Rs as follows:

- Cognitive/**review**: keywords are identified, information is coded through, for example, mnemonics and notes are made.
- Associative/**remember**: information is transferred from the working- to the short-term then long-term memory.
- Autonomous/**recall**: thinking is applied to give answers in a range of contexts. As the assignments become more complex and challenging, the higher order thinking skills are applied.

DON'T FORGET

Get into the habit of using all three stages: cognitive/**review** associative/**remember** autonomous/**recall**.

THE 3RS IN PRACTICE – THE IDEAL STUDY HOUR 1

Study sessions need to be planned to make them as interesting and effective as possible. Few people can maintain their concentration over long periods of time. In classes, teachers will often vary tasks throughout the lesson to help you remain interested and motivated. Similarly, your study session should be broken down into segments with time to focus on each of the **review**, **remember** and **recall** processes.

'TO DO LESS CAN BE TO DO MORE'

We're not saying that you should study less – just that you should keep study periods short to make them more effective. To have a productive study hour, split it into smaller segments – just like teachers do in class. That way, you'll stop your mind wandering and you won't be in danger of becoming bored.

In an **ideal study hour** you **review** the information you are going to learn by making notes and gathering prompts. You then use these notes and prompts to help you **remember** the information by committing it first to your short-term memory, and then to your long-term memory. Finally, you use the **recall** process to select the information you need from the prompts to answer specific questions.

If you spend long periods of time reading books or notes, you'll come to rely on these to prompt your memory. As you won't have the books or notes with you in the exam, you need to help your brain to make these connections without seeing them. Here's how. In an ideal study hour you should do the following:

- **Review** the information.
- Test what you have learned and **remembered using prompts**.
- **Recall** and practise applying the information through homework or past exam paper questions.

Not everyone will spend the same time on each activity for a number of reasons. You might find it easier to study if you are really interested in a subject, or you might prefer to use a style of learning that takes more time.

STUDY SUPPORT

Involve your helpers

You can involve your study supporters in your ideal study hour – particularly during the **remember** and **recall** sections – to help you check how much you have learned. They can also help you with the timings and can make sure that your study area is well lit and not too noisy, and that you will be left in peace!

EXAMPLE

The following table suggests some of the timings you could allocate to different types of activities.

1 Preparation	2 Review	3 Have a break	4 Remember/recall previous work	5 Have a break	6 Daily recall check
Gather together all your study materials.	**Review** your notes/ books to: • learn something new • draw a **mind-map** • write notes, order your thoughts • learn from a new resource.	Break. Have a drink.	**Remember/recall** Look over notes and reflect and test how much you remember from: • yesterday • last week • last month.	Break. Relax.	**Remember/recall** Reflect and test yourself on what you did in the 20-minute section.
5 minutes	20 minutes	5 minutes	15 minutes	5 minutes	10 minutes

SEGMENT 1 – PREPARATION (5 MINUTES)

The first part of your ideal study hour should be spent preparing for the rest of the hour, and should not take more than about five minutes. During this short segment, do the following:

- Put your clock or watch where you can see it easily.
- Get yourself ready for studying by thinking through what you are planning to do and gather all the equipment, books and notes that you will need in the study hour.
- Check that you are comfortable. If you are uncomfortable, you will waste a lot of time and mental energy shuffling about in your seat. You don't want to be stiff at the end of the study hour if you've been sitting in an awkward position.
- If you like working with music, select appropriate music to listen to or make sure you can study quietly, without being disturbed.
- Make sure that you have adequate lighting so you don't strain your eyes.

DON'T FORGET +

This is just a guide. Have a go at making your own version.

DON'T FORGET +

There will be times when you start a piece of work and get really absorbed in it. When this happens, just carry on working or you might lose your flow of thought. If you find you are starting to daydream, lose focus or have spent the last five minutes doing nothing, then take a break and return to it refreshed.

THINGS TO DO AND THINK ABOUT

Now review your study environment. Do you need to change it at all to make your study time work better for you?

THE 3RS IN PRACTICE – THE IDEAL STUDY HOUR 2

SEGMENT 2 – REVIEW: LEARNING NEW INFORMATION (20 MINUTES)

The second segment is probably the most difficult part of your study hour. You should:

- gather information by reviewing books, notes and internet articles
- identify key points
- create your own brief study notes
- devise memory prompts
- learn your notes and prompts.

Your study notes should be laid out in an attractive way so that you want to read them and they are easy to read. You will need to work out your own system of prompts, such as underlining words and phrases, developing mnemonics and rhymes and drawing diagrams. (These will be covered in more detail in the 'Remember' chapter on page 50.) By using these prompts, you can then learn and apply the information in the **remember** and **recall** segment of the study hour using techniques such as:

- **look/cover/write/check**
- reciting facts and information
- drawing study posters for your room.

SEGMENT 3 – HAVE A BREAK (5 MINUTES)

The third segment is a short one. Get up, move about, rearrange your books ready for the next part of the session and get a drink or something to nibble. Change your music if necessary to suit the type of work you are about to do.

DON'T FORGET

You only have a five minute break – don't let it extend to 10 or 15 minutes!

SEGMENT 4 – REMEMBER/RECALL PREVIOUS WORK (15 MINUTES)

The fourth segment of your study hour is very important. Look over your study notes from earlier study sessions and check whether you still **remember** and **recall** the relevant information. Use your reflective thinking for this – look at the keywords and check that your brain has made the connections that link these words to the relevant bank of information. You should draw up a schedule to ensure that you look over notes from the previous week, month and earlier months. This will help you to commit information to your long-term memory.

If you find that there is something you can't remember, make a note of it in a notebook, or keep a **To Learn** folder in your computer or phone. Spend some time trying to remember it. Test yourself in another week to check whether you have learned it. If you have remembered it, then you can score it off in your notebook or delete it from your **To Learn** folder. If you haven't learned it, repeat the process until you do.

To make this part of the process more realistic, answer revision questions and set out your answers as if you were working under exam conditions and time limits.

SEGMENT 5 – HAVE A BREAK (5 MINUTES)

The fifth segment is another short one. Get up again and move about, rearrange your books, get a drink or something to nibble or change your music again. Nearly there – just remember to come back for the last 10 minutes...

SEGMENT 6 – DAILY RECALL CHECK (10 MINUTES)

Start the sixth and final segment of your study hour with reflective thinking. What you can remember from the second segment? Test yourself to see if you can recall the work you've done. If you can't, go over it again in your next study session. During this time, you are starting to put items into your short-term and long-term memory – making the information **your** information and the learning **your** learning!

If you have time and can do a second study hour, you should use the same basic structure, but miss out the 15-minute **recall** section because you've already done this. Anything you had difficulty remembering in the first hour could be revisited in this last 10-minute section.

THINGS TO DO AND THINK ABOUT

Plan your study for the week for your favourite subject using the ideal study hour format. At the end of the week, try to remember and recall what you learned on the first day. How did you get on? Now do the same for your other subjects.

STUDY SUPPORT

Ask your study supporters to help you check your learning during the last 10-minute daily recall segment.

DON'T FORGET

Try to look over previous work every two or three months to keep it active in your brain so that you don't forget it. You might also be able to use this information to help you learn more recent work.

TOP TIP

Put your watch or a clock where you can easily see it.

STUDY PLAN

A good study **plan** is the key to effective learning. It will help you to systematically plan your work and it will also help to motivate you when you see the amount of work that you've covered in each subject. We've included an exemplar study plan here, but remember that this is only a suggestion, and that you can adapt it to suit your own needs.

An important part of any study plan is the amount of time spent on study. This will vary depending on who you are and the subjects that you're doing. An optimum time for students in the senior phase (S4, 5, 6) is around two hours per session. This gives you enough time to commit more detailed information to the long-term memory so you can do more challenging activities in class and be better prepared for assignments.

Study plans also help you to allocate time for ongoing work such as homework and revision. The first priority for each session must be to complete homework. This will determine how much time is left available for revision.

+ DON'T FORGET

Homework is a form of study.

HOW OFTEN?

If you're really serious about doing well in your exams, you should be planning about five sessions per week. It's up to you when you do them. Some people prefer working Monday to Friday, while others prefer to have Friday and Saturday free and work Sunday to Thursday.

LEISURE AND SOCIAL EVENTS

Remember to include time for leisure and social events in the plan. You need opportunities to relax, even while the exams are going on or when you are finishing portfolio and added value work. If you don't have time off, you'll probably get over-tired, lose perspective and increase the stress you are under. With an effective plan you should be able to meet your social commitments without feeling guilty that you are not at home studying and working.

FLEXIBILITY

Even when you've drawn up your plan, be flexible with it. The plan is only a guide and a method of monitoring. Things happen in life that we have to respond to. Missing one or two days is not the end of the world. If you find it difficult to stick to your plan, adapt it. If your plan is too ambitious, review it and start again. Start small. It is better to do even ten minutes per night than nothing at all, and all these ten minutes will add up.

PRIORITISE

Use your study plan to set your priorities. Fill in any deadlines or test dates well in advance. Then fill in social, family or sporting events. Your revision should fit in around these things.

+ DON'T FORGET

The **review/remember/recall** process should be built into the study plan. In particular, use **remember** and **recall** sessions to look over work done in the earlier parts of the course.

+ DON'T FORGET

To make learning most effective, look over your work frequently. This could be at the end of the session or day, after a week, after a month and after three months. Of course, this will depend on how easy or hard the piece of work is to remember, and it will vary according to individual needs.

STUDY SUPPORT

Let your study supporters look at your study plan so that they know when you're planning to work and can be there to encourage you. They can also help you to adapt the plan if it's too demanding or not demanding enough.

MONTHLY STUDY PLAN

Your school might provide you with a template for a study plan. Don't forget that this will probably include holidays.

Use colour and pictures to make it more interesting and easier to read.

Try to revise each subject at least once a week or, if you have more than five subjects, at least once every two weeks. During the subject revision time, try to use the **ideal study hour** and **3Rs** format. Arrange all your notes by subject, and keep everything filed properly.

EXAMPLE

Monthly study plan

		Session 1	Session 2	Session 3	Session 4	Session 5
Week beginning 5 September	H/work	Maths p34–5	English poetry	Maths p35–6 Geography p5	English	Maths Ex 4 Biology p26 a, b
	Revision	French	Maths	English	Geography	Biology
	Leisure	Swimming		Visit Gran	Watch match on TV	
Week beginning 12 September	H/work	Maths Finish Ex 5	English Learn quotes French vocabulary	Maths Finish Ex 6	English spelling (Do on Wed)	Biology Finish diagram
	Revision	French	Maths Geography	English		Biology
	Leisure	Swimming		Visit Gran	My birthday	Friends staying overnight
Week beginning 19 September	H/work	Geography Revise – river test	Geography Revise – river test	Maths p43–44	English spelling	French Verbs
	Revision	French	Maths	English	Geography	Biology
	Leisure	Swimming		Visit Gran		Going to friend's house
Week beginning 26 September	H/work	English folio draft	Maths p46–47	French Oral prep	Geography Review test performance	Learn mushroom diagram
	Revision	French	Maths Biology	English	Geography	
	Leisure	Swimming		Visit Gran		Scouts' weekend

HOW GOOD ARE YOUR ORGANISATIONAL SKILLS?

Are you the type of person who tidies up after themselves or is your bedroom floor covered in mounds of clothes, books, shoes and stuff? Some people are naturally tidy and like making lists and arranging things. Others aren't and don't.

People who are well organised can find it fairly easy to fill in a study plan. A lot of people find this very hard, but it is really important that you develop and monitor your programme and progress.

Even if you find it hard try to stick with it. Remember – you don't have to use the format shown above. Make up your own plan and decorate it with pictures or photos if it encourages you to look at it and makes it more fun. Keep it on your computer desktop, on your phone or print it out and put it on your bedroom wall. You could do it as a weekly programme or a monthly programme. You could even make up a spreadsheet on your computer. Choose whatever works best for you.

DON'T FORGET

Be careful not to spend more time making up your plan than you do studying!

THINGS TO DO AND THINK ABOUT

Make up your own study plan. You can use the example above as a template, or you can create your own. Try to make it look so good that you will want to look at it and fill it out.

SETTING REALISTIC GOALS AND TARGETS

It is important for your confidence and progress that you set **short-** and **longer-term targets** that are achievable. These targets will be determined, for example, by the class or group you are in, by results in previous tests or exams, or by course entry requirements (which can include practical experience in addition to formal academic qualifications).

Targets should be **SMARTER**. This mnemonic means:

Specific to your needs
Measurable
Achievable
Realistic
Timescale
Evaluate
Recorded

SPECIFIC

Specific targets relate directly to the **grades** you want to achieve for your essays, tests and assignments, and for the overall course award. If you are aware of your strengths and weaknesses, you can ensure that your study programme plays on your strengths and improves your weaknesses.

MEASURABLE

Evaluate your strengths and weaknesses on an ongoing basis as you work through your course, and you will gradually improve and achieve better results. Use techniques such as **look/cover/write/check** (see page 54) in your assignment drafts and re-drafts, or practise doing past exam papers to **measure** how you are progressing throughout the course.

ACHIEVABLE

It is vitally important for your confidence and motivation to make sure that you can actually achieve your targets. Setting targets that are too hard can lead to demotivation and you might start to feel that the course is too difficult for you.

On the other hand, you need to make sure your targets are not set too low, or you might fool yourself into thinking you are doing well when you are not really stretching yourself and achieving to the best of your ability. Set **achievable** weekly targets so you can see that you are continually and steadily learning the materials.

REALISTIC

Set your targets to fit in with the course timetable and your personal life. There are only a certain number of hours available for study after you've accounted for all the other things in life (like eating and sleeping), and you need to be **realistic** about how many hours you can actually devote to your study, and how much you can achieve in that time.

If you know you are going on holiday or have a commitment, don't plan a lot of study for that time. It will only make you feel guilty and your mind probably won't be on studying anyway. Instead do a little extra before and after, and you will be able to fulfil your commitment or enjoy your holiday and fully focus on the task in hand.

Most importantly, make sure you are actually able to reach your targets. Seek the advice and reassurance of your teacher or tutor. After all, there is no point in trying to answer a past paper question or write your portfolio before you have completed that part of the course work!

TIMESCALE

To learn effectively, you need to commit the materials to your short-term and long-term memory right through the course, and not just cram them into your short-term memory before a test. Combine the **review/remember/**

recall process with a well-planned study programme and you should be well-prepared for all your exams and assignments. Use the **ideal study hour** format and a **monthly study plan** to support this.

EVALUATE

Be honest with yourself about what you know well, what you sort of know, what you are not so sure of and/or what you really don't know. Once you know your strengths and weaknesses, go over the things you are weaker in and evaluate your performance on a regular basis until you are confident that you're improving.

RECORDED

Write down what you have learned and the time you have spent studying. Draw up a chart for your wall or computer or use a diary and actually **record** what you have done. It will boost your confidence to see how much you have covered, and you'll go into the test feeling prepared.

DON'T FORGET

Write out your weekly targets and tick them off when you achieve them. This helps you to appreciate the progress you are making:

'It is better to take many small steps in the right direction than to make a great leap forward only to stumble backward.' *(Louis Sachar)*

THINGS TO DO AND THINK ABOUT

If you find it hard to get into a study routine, complete the following table or use it to create a bar or line **graph**. Try to study five times per week for up to two hours per session. Record how much time you spend in each study session. Set a weekly target, but be realistic. If you don't study much just now, start off by setting your target for two hours 30 minutes per week (30 minutes per session) or five hours per week (one hour per session) and work it up to 10 hours per week.

Set up a routine that works for you. Less is better than nothing at all! If you need to, start off small and build it up.

STUDY SUPPORT

Ask your study supporters to help you set and monitor your targets.

	Monday	Tuesday	Wednesday	Thursday	Friday	Saturday	Sunday	Weekly target	Hours achieved
Week 1								10 hours	
Week 2								10 hours	
Week 3								10 hours	
Week 4								10 hours	

Record of work covered

MAKING NOTES – KEYWORDS 1

Review is the first stage in the 3Rs process. In the review stage, you have to identify keywords in your notes or texts and turn them into memory prompts that will help your brain to recreate and recall the more in-depth, detailed information you need for your exams and assignments. We will explore a number of techniques in this chapter to help you do this.

REVIEWING AND ACTIVE STUDY

For many learners, reviewing is the most difficult part of the study process. People are often unaware of study skills or they don't use them in their own programme.

Spending considerable amounts of time simply reading over notes again and again may work for a few people, but for most this is a slow method and often the learner does not check if they can recall the information without the texts in front of them.

Active study involves reading the materials and doing something with them – making your brain work to create the connections between the key points and banks of associated information. This could be making notes, using symbols or checking if the information can be recalled. It's almost like using shortened codes to access larger areas of information.

REVIEWING AND REFLECTIVE THINKING

Reflecting on the key points covered in class or in texts starts the active study process. It encourages the brain to sift through large volumes of information and start to organise it. It creates links and puts information into categories and identifies the key points. For example, in algebra, connections will be made between equations, number work, brackets, denominator, numerator and so on. This bank of information will help you to solve equations.

During the review process, your brain significantly **compresses this information** into **key points**, which act as **memory prompts**. Once your brain becomes familiar with these prompts you will be able to **use them in context** to build up the big picture, producing something similar to the original text.

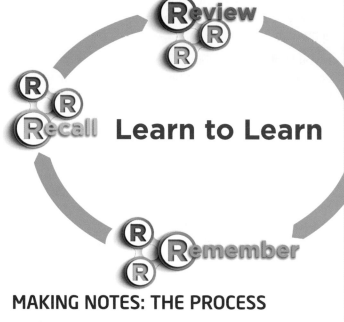

Learn to Learn

MAKING NOTES: THE PROCESS

The first challenge in the review process is to learn how to make your own brief notes from longer texts such as class handouts and books. This involves linking several key stages:

1. Follow the signposts to find **key points** in the original texts.
2. Mark the **keywords**. This could be **subject-specific vocabulary** – words that have a specific or technical meaning in a particular subject. Use highlighter pens, underlining or written comments to mark them clearly. You'll use these key points in your own notes.
3. Use **prompts**, such as mnemonics, rhymes, abbreviations and **text language**, mind-maps and **spider diagrams**.
4. Make notes look **attractive** and easy to read over.
5. **Paraphrase** – **do not plagiarise** or use quotations without acknowledging them.

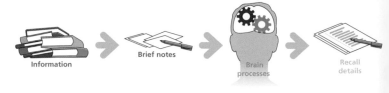

Information → Brief notes → Brain processes → Recall details

FOLLOW THE SIGNPOSTS TO FIND KEYWORDS

Authors often use a range of techniques to signpost keywords for you. When you are reading and reviewing a text, look out for the following:

- Phrases such as 'It is important...'
- Chapter summaries (when the content of the chapter is introduced at the beginning of the chapter) and chapter conclusions (when all the keywords are summarised at the end of the chapter).
- Words and worked examples in shaded boxes.
- Words that are underlined, in **bold** or *italic print* or in larger print.
- Subheadings that use key words or phrases to summarise the content which follows.

ACTIVITY

Choose a textbook. Look at the last few paragraphs in the chapter. Does it summarise the material in the chapter? Repeat the task with different textbooks.

IDENTIFY KEYWORDS 1

Many students overdo the use of both underlining and highlighting. If you underline or highlight entire paragraphs, your brain won't be able to extract the information quickly or identify the keywords.

Identifying and using keywords and subject-specific vocabulary is really important because teachers will award marks for them in answers. It is a fundamental technique that everybody should develop. Don't worry if you don't find this easy – we've got some techniques to help you.

ACTIVITY

Look through some textbooks to find examples of keywords that have been highlighted in a box or a coloured background. Maths books tend to use this method to present a new concept and a worked example of that concept. If you have a maths book, look through it to identify an example of this.

DON'T FORGET

In SQA exams and assessments, markers will look for key words and phrases in answers. Marks will be awarded for using these appropriately.

The activities here and on the next few pages will help you get to grips with identifying keywords in passages of text.

In the following passage about alcohol, start by underlining the keywords one paragraph at a time. This will help to build up your confidence in this key skill.

ACTIVITY

Alcohol passage

For this task imagine that you have been asked to give a brief talk on alcohol.

In the following passage, underline what you think are the keywords.

Alcohol is a chemical substance which affects the central nervous system (CNS). It is called a depressant drug as it slows down the CNS. Drinking alcohol affects the way the brain functions and there are a range of side effects on the body. The amount drunk, the time period, whether the person has had a meal before starting to drink, their age and their physical size can all affect the intensity of the side effects.

As the amount of alcohol in the body increases, the body goes through a range of side effects. These can start with feeling relaxed and happy to slurred speech, blurred vision and coordination problems, to vomiting then unconsciousness and even death.

Death can also occur by choking on vomit. An unconscious drunk person should be placed in the recovery position.

THINGS TO DO AND THINK ABOUT

Now look at an example of a response to this task on the next page, where the keywords have been underlined.

MAKING NOTES – KEYWORDS 2

IDENTIFY KEYWORDS 2

ACTIVITY

Alcohol passage – suggested keywords

The following example shows one response to this task, and includes the reasons for underlining those specific keywords. But don't worry – this is not the 'correct' or definitive answer and you haven't failed the task if your keywords are not the same.

EXAMPLE

Alcohol is a <u>chemical substance</u> which affects the central nervous system (<u>CNS</u>). It is called a <u>depressant drug</u> as it <u>slows</u> down the CNS. Drinking alcohol affects the way the <u>brain functions</u> and there are a range of <u>side effects</u> on the body. The <u>amount</u> drunk, the <u>time</u> period, whether the person has had a <u>meal</u> before starting to drink, their <u>age</u> and their physical <u>size</u> can all affect the <u>intensity</u> of the side effects.

As the amount of alcohol in the body increases, the body goes through a range of side effects. These can start with feeling <u>relaxed</u> and <u>happy</u> to <u>slurred speech</u>, <u>blurred vision</u> and <u>coordination problems</u> to <u>vomiting</u> then <u>unconsciousness</u> and even <u>death</u>.

Death can also occur by choking on <u>vomit</u>. An unconscious drunk person should be placed in the <u>recovery position</u>.

Reasons For Underlining The Selected Words

<u>Chemical substance</u> and <u>CNS</u> state the definition of a drug. <u>CNS</u> is underlined instead of Central Nervous System to help with familiarity of the initials and the phrase. Using initials like this can save time in exams and keep the number of words down if you are working to a word limit in an assignment. Wherever you use this technique, make sure that on the first occasion you use the phrase, you always give the full phrase first, followed by the initials.

<u>Depressant</u> and <u>slows</u> describes how the drug works.

<u>Brain functions</u> highlights the fact that alcohol has an effect on the brain.

<u>Side effects</u> shows that there are a range of different impacts on the brain.

<u>Amount</u>, <u>time</u>, <u>meal</u>, <u>age</u>, <u>size</u> all relate to the <u>intensity</u> of the effects of the drug – how drunk the person is.

<u>Relaxed</u>, <u>happy</u>, <u>slurred speech</u>, <u>blurred vision</u>, <u>coordination problems</u>, <u>vomiting</u>, <u>unconsciousness</u> and <u>death</u> all describe the side effects.

<u>Vomit</u> and <u>recovery position</u> relate to first aid procedures and essential knowledge for everyone. You could use them if you are discussing social responsibility in an exam.

Grouping Keywords

If the keywords are related, group them together and give them a heading to help your brain connect these pieces of information. For example, using the text from the previous task, you could have the following groups:

- Definitions: chemical substance, (CNS), depressant drug
- Drunkenness: amount, time, meal, age, size, intensity
- Side effects: relaxed, happy, slurred speech, blurred vision, coordination problems, vomiting, unconsciousness, death
- First aid: vomit, recovery position

These group headings help your brain to organise and put information into useful categories. For example, you might be asked for a definition of the effects of alcohol. The items listed under **definitions** in your notes would give you some depth and detail to structure your answer around. Depending on the question, you could then add in some of the other keywords if relevant.

In an exam or assignment, you should be able to use the keywords you have underlined as prompts to help you to build up a fuller, more detailed response. Try out the following task for the 'Alcohol' passage.

THINGS TO DO AND THINK ABOUT

1. Look again at the keywords you underlined in the passage and compare these to the keywords underlined in the example. From the four phrases below, choose the phrase that best applies to what you did and then complete it with your own comment.

   I underlined fewer keywords than the example because

   _____

   I underlined about the same amount of keywords as the example because

   _____

   I underlined more keywords than the example because

   _____

   I underlined different keywords from the example because

   _____

   Have you underlined (circle the one which applies most):

   - too many keywords?
   - just about the right amount of keywords?
   - too few keywords ?

2. Write down the keywords on a sheet of paper. Using the paper as a prompt, deliver a talk on alcohol to a friend or family member, or say it out loud to yourself in front of a mirror.

   - Were you able to build up the bigger picture using the keywords as prompts?
   - Did you need more information? If you did, was this because you couldn't remember what the keywords represented?
   - Repeat the talk again – was it easier the second time?

3. Find a passage on a topic that really interests you and underline the keywords. Again, write down the keywords on a sheet of paper and use this as a prompt to deliver a talk. Was it easier to do with a topic that you liked and knew more about?

TOP TIP

If you learn the keywords, you will be able to remember the information to explain or discuss in an exam.

DON'T FORGET

Being able to identify keywords is crucial for effective study. If this is an area you are weak in, use your own study notes to practise.

STUDY SUPPORT

Involve your study supporters in these tasks.

MAKING NOTES – USING PROMPTS 1

USE KEYWORD PROMPTS

The next step is to turn your keywords into memory prompts that will help your brain to recreate and recall the more in-depth, detailed information you need for your exams and assignments. Over the next few sections we'll explain how you can do this by using the following techniques:

- adding definitions
- mnemonics
- rhymes and rhythms
- abbreviations and symbols
- mind-maps and spider diagrams
- flow charts
- diagrams and graphs
- chunking.

The more varied and fun the memory prompts are, the easier it will be to learn them and recall the information.

The challenge is to include a range of these prompts in your study, and to choose the ones that are most effective at helping you to learn different types of information.

DON'T FORGET

Your brain doesn't like to be bored by processing the same type of information again and again – it needs to be stimulated if it is to work at its best.

ADDING DEFINITIONS

In reflective thinking, recalling keywords triggers your brain to remember associated banks of information. Adding definitions to the keywords means that the associated information is much more concise. For example, the definition for 'alliteration' is 'repetition of a consonant or sound at the beginning of a group of words'. If you include the definition after the keywords, it lets the reader know that you have a good understanding of the word.

EXAMPLE

The use of alliteration, *repetition of a consonant or sound at the beginning of a group of words*, is particularly effective as the harsh sound of the letter 'c' in 'cold clay clads his coffin' emphasises the grimness of the description.

This detail may result in more marks being awarded as you have shown a deep, thorough understanding.

Where Will I Find Definitions?

Some keywords require very precise definitions, particularly in science – for example, velocity = the speed of something in a particular direction.

Initially, your teacher will give you definitions and you will find them in your books, notes and glossaries. Once you get into the habit of learning and using definitions for some words, you may be able to make up your own from your banks of information.

TOP TIP

Try to get into the habit of adding definitions to your keywords whenever you can.

MNEMONICS

Mnemonics use letters, words or phrases to help prompt the memory.

The first letter of each word on the list forms a sentence or a word. (This can also help you to remember the order of the items.) The prompt words or sentences do not have to be related in any way to the topic. In fact, sometimes the more ridiculous the prompt is, the easier it is to remember (and more fun).

Acronyms

An acronym is a specific type of mnemonic that uses the initial letters of a phrase to form a word. Acronyms are good for remembering lists, particularly if you need to remember them in a certain order.

Here are some examples of mnemonics:

EXAMPLE

The colours of the rainbow are: **r**ed, **o**range, **y**ellow, **g**reen, **b**lue, **i**ndigo, **v**iolet.

A famous mnemonic for this is: **R**ichard **O**f **Y**ork **G**ave **B**attle **I**n **V**ain.

An alternative is **ROY G BIV**.

EXAMPLE

The first aid treatment for a twisted ankle is: **r**est the injury, apply **i**ce to it, bandage the joint to **c**ompress it, **e**levate (raise) it.

This can be shortened to:
Rest, **I**ce, **C**ompression, **E**levation, to create the acronym **RICE**.

ACTIVITY

Look at the list of planets below. Make up your own mnemonic to learn the planets and their order from the sun. An example is given. You can use some of these words in your own version if you wish – but not all of them!

The planets that orbit the sun are (in order from the sun):
Mercury, Venus, Earth, Mars, Jupiter, Saturn, Uranus, Neptune.

An example would be:
My **V**ery **E**asy **M**ethod **J**ust **S**peeds **U**p **N**aming

Spelling

You can also use mnemonics or easy-to-remember phrases to improve your spelling and remember spelling rules:

- RHYTHM – **r**hythm **h**elps **y**our **t**wo **h**ips **m**ove
- OCEAN – **o**nly **c**ats' **e**yes **a**re **n**arrow
- BECAUSE – **b**ig **e**lephants **c**an **a**lways **u**nderstand **s**mall **e**lephants
- BEAUTIFUL – **b**ig **e**lephants **a**re **u**gly
- RECEIVE – **I** before **E** except after **C**
- POTASSIUM – one **t**ea and two **s**ugars
- DESERT or DESSERT – desert (like the Sahara) has one S, dessert (like apple crumble) has two and you always want two desserts.

ACTIVITY

Go to the dictionary or your notes and select a word you have difficulty spelling. Make up a mnemonic for it – either a phrase or a word. Use this to try to remember it. Check again after half an hour to find out if you can still remember it.

Traditional Sayings And Phrases

Some phrases and sayings have been used as mnemonics by generations of people. One well-known example reminds people whether to put their clocks forward or back an hour at the start and end of British Summer Time:

EXAMPLE

When British Summer Time officially starts (at the end of March, in spring) the clocks go forward an hour. When British Summer Time officially ends (at the end of October, in autumn) the clocks go back an hour.

The phrase that most people use to remember whether the clocks go back or forward is:

Spring forward, fall back.
(Fall is the American term for autumn.)

THINGS TO DO AND THINK ABOUT

Can you think of any mnemonics that you learned years ago, perhaps in primary school? If so, then this has been a very effective method of learning for you. Make sure you continue to use it during the review part of your study.

Teachers in some subjects will give you mnemonics to help you learn particular pieces of work. It is worth learning these as they are recognised as being effective in exams. Many people remember the mnemonics years after they learned them in class.

MAKING NOTES – USING PROMPTS 2

Days in each month

Thirty days hath September,
April, June and November,
All the rest have thirty-one,
Excepting February alone,
Which has twenty-eight days clear,
And twenty-nine in each leap year.

RHYMES AND RHYTHMS

Rhymes can also be a really useful memory prompt. Left is a very well-known rhyme that many people use to remember the number of days in each month. You probably know it yourself.

Rhymes are easy to remember because they have a rhythm or beat to them. Many learners add a rhythm to phrases or longer words as they go over them in their minds. Some people even put the words to music from their favourite songs. These rhythms become another prompt which the brain uses to try to recall information. This is particularly useful for auditory and kinaesthetic learners.

ABBREVIATIONS AND SYMBOLS

When you are writing your own notes, try using common **abbreviations and symbols** such as:

@ instead of 'at'	= instead of 'equals'	→ instead of 'leads to'

If you use text language, include that in your note-taking where appropriate. You can always make up your own abbreviations when you are taking notes. Just remember not to use your own abbreviations in exams and assignments, but to write phrases in full or use standard abbreviations.

Although you should always try to write text language out in full in an exam, use abbreviations if you are struggling for time – especially for phrases that you're using a lot. The first time you write out a phrase, write the abbreviation for it in brackets directly after it – for example, as on page 37 where **C**entral **N**ervous **S**ystem is abbreviated or shortened to **CNS**. You can then just use the abbreviation after that, because your examiner will know what you mean. Be careful, however, not to use abbreviations for too many words or phrases, because that could make it difficult for your examiner to follow the meaning of the passage.

✚ DON'T FORGET

If you use an abbreviation in an essay or an exam, write it out in full the first time you use it and put the abbreviation in brackets directly after it.

For example: **C**entral **N**ervous **S**ystem (CNS) or **P**reparation, **A**ction, **R**ecovery (PAR).

MIND-MAPS AND SPIDER DIAGRAMS

Mind-maps and spider diagrams are drawings that have a **central theme**, with **related information** branching out from this theme. Research has shown that the brain is very efficient at recognising and processing the information laid out in this format. It allows the thought process to flow through the items, making links between them.

Spider diagrams are the most basic form of this technique. They simply show a central theme with the ideas radiating out on the strands.

Mind-maps are more complicated. Here are some of the most important rules for mind-mapping, along with some suggestions and ideas for you to try out.

When you create a mind-map, keep the following points in mind:

- Start with a **keyword** or theme at the centre.
- Start the first **branch** (or **strand**) at one o'clock and **work round clockwise**. The strands radiate out from the centre. Each strand represents **one theme** or idea which is a subset of the keyword at the centre.
- Identify each strand or sub-strand clearly with a word or a symbol.
- Put the more important points on the part of the strand nearest the centre.
- Make sure the strands don't have any breaks.

To help make the mind-map more memorable:

- use **different colours** for each strand
- use **symbols**, **pictures** or **abbreviations** instead of words (particularly useful for visual learners)
- use **dotted lines** to link related strands
- make the **strand thicker** at the **centre**, and thinner towards the outer branches.

To the right is an example of a mind-map based on the topic of 'Healthy Me':

FLOW CHARTS

Flow charts also link together related pieces of information. This can be particularly useful for problem-solving activities or discussions. For example, if your mobile phone doesn't work, you will probably go through the process seen in the flow chart to the right.

The flow chart shows how you solve that problem. Use flow charts in your study notes to show the stages in sequential processes and the range of possible outcomes. You can also use this process to solve problems by starting with the main issue and asking questions so that you can consider the various options and decide upon the best one.

THINGS TO DO AND THINK ABOUT

1. Look through your books and notes for examples of abbreviations.

2. Choose a subject that contains complicated phrases or repeats phrases frequently. Make up your own abbreviations for these phrases.

3. Create your own 'Healthy Me' mind-map using your own key points and strand headings. (You can use some of the strand headings from the example, if you want.)

4. Create your own mind-map or flow chart with 'You' as the central theme. Use family, friends, hobbies, favourite food/colours/music and so on, as the strands.

DON'T FORGET

Your mind-maps, spider diagrams and flow charts can be used to link information to a keyword or to cover a whole topic. Adapt these techniques to suit how your brain works.

MAKING NOTES – USING PROMPTS 3

DIAGRAMS AND GRAPHS

Diagrams and graphs that are labelled with **keywords** can be quick to draw, are easy to learn, contain a lot of information and can be used to answer questions. They are particularly useful in the sciences, where they are used to identify objects and also to show relationships in equations.

When you are studying and writing assessment answers, you can use diagrams and graphs to:

1. **recall** information and **rewrite** it as text

2. **answer the question** (points can be awarded for well-labelled diagrams).

You can use a diagram to augment your written answer. This takes much less time than writing a long explanation – a useful tactic if time is short in an exam, or if you are getting close to your word limit.

Left is an example of a labelled diagram and an example of a graph from a physics book.

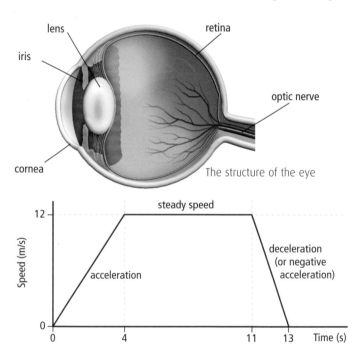

The structure of the eye

CHUNKING

Chunking is a study technique that breaks information down into small chunks or parts. It can be used to help the memory in both number and writing work. It's easier and more effective to learn little bits of information over a longer period than it is to learn it all at once – especially just before a test! You can use chunking to help with your study planning.

Plan your study by **doing a little, often**. For example, imagine that on Monday you are given twelve words to learn for French or German for Thursday. Instead of trying to learn all twelve words on Wednesday night, learn four new words on Monday, four on Tuesday and four on Wednesday, checking each evening what you have learned the night before.

Similarly, when you are learning how to spell a new word, try breaking it down into sections. For example, photosynthesis could be broken down into photo-syn-thesis or photo-synthesis depending on what you find easiest. Cinematography could become cinema-to-graphy or cinema-to-gra-phy.

One example of chunking is the way you remember telephone numbers. Most people will break down an eleven digit number into smaller chunks. For example, the number for a landline starts with an area code (usually a four or five digit number) which can be remembered in one chunk. The second part of the number (six or seven digits) can be remembered in one chunk, or in two groups, for example:
01645 – 432567 or 01645 – 432 – 567.

You can also use chunking when you are writing out your study notes. It helps you to see the key points clearly and to find information quickly. Chunked notes would include:

- bullet point lists of key points and ideas
- subheadings
- short sentences with one or two ideas per sentence
- short paragraphs.

Breaking up text by using bullet points and subheadings will help your brain to recognise the format and be able to pick out the keywords more easily. If you're a visual learner, picturing the layout will often help you to remember the key points.

DON'T FORGET

If you automatically break down numbers into chunks, then you're already chunking without realising it. Use this skill when you study.

ACTIVITY

Choose difficult words from your subject material or the dictionary and break them down into smaller chunks before trying to learn them.

ACTIVITY

Make a bullet point list using text you have chosen from your notes or a textbook.

Next, make subheadings using the same text (or choose a different text if you prefer).

MAKE NOTES LOOK ATTRACTIVE AND EASY TO READ

Make your notes look interesting. Use different coloured pens and pencils, pictures, diagrams and highlighter pens to stimulate your brain and make learning enjoyable.

Leave lines between different topics and use headings so that you can see at a glance what is on the page.

PARAPHRASE, DON'T PLAGIARISE

Paraphrasing is when you take what someone else has said or written and you put into your own words. This can make things easier to remember.

However, if you're writing an essay or an exam answer, you might be marked more highly if you can give an exact **quote**. If you do this, you need to enclose the quote within 'quotation marks' and give the name of the original author. Depending on the context, you might also need to give the title of the book or the article where the quote appears.

You must not plagiarise, or try to pass off someone else's work as your own. If you do this, you run the risk of having your work rejected completely. Most universities will expel any students who plagiarise in essays. Always acknowledge the original author.

THINGS TO DO AND THINK ABOUT

Don't use the same methods for making notes all the time, or your brain will get bored of seeing the same thing. The brain needs stimulation so use the range of chunking techniques listed above. Use different symbols for your bullet points to keep your brain interested.

USING AND PRACTISING STUDY SKILLS

You have now learned how to turn your keywords into memory prompts that will help your brain to recreate and recall the more in-depth, detailed information you need for your exams and assignments. You did this by learning about the following techniques:

- underlining and highlighting keywords and topics
- mnemonics
- rhymes and rhythms
- abbreviations and symbols
- mind-maps and spider diagrams
- flow charts
- diagrams and graphs
- chunking.

The next step is to practise using these techniques by building them into your study plan. If you commit to using them regularly, you'll find, after a while, that you will use them automatically both in your study and in your exams and assignments.

THE STUDY SKILLS PROCESS

When you are building your study plan, remember to consider the three-stage study skill process. It looks like this:

The cognitive/learning stage →

  The associative/practice stage →

    The autonomous/automatic stage

This table shows how this three-stage skill process fits in with the **3Rs** process.

Cognitive stage	Review	Information is condensed into study notes with keywords, mnemonics, and so on.
Associative stage	Remember	Information is transferred and stored in the short- then long-term memory.
Autonomous stage	Recall	Appropriate knowledge is selected, adapted and applied to understand and answer questions.

Try to use these skills as part of your routine along with the **SMARTER** targets discussed on pages 34–35.

ACTIVITY

Draw up a table like the one shown below, either using paper and pen or a computer. Put a tick in the box for all the types of study techniques you use over the next four weeks for your favourite subject. At the end of week 4 enter one of the following:

☺   if you have used the technique well.

😐   if you have used it but could have used it a bit more.

☹   if you haven't used it but you now realise that there were opportunities to use it.

	Week 1	Week 2	Week 3	Week 4	Evaluation
Underlining keywords/topics					
Using a highlighter to show keywords/topics					
Mnemonics					
Rhymes					
Abbreviations and symbols					
Mind-maps					
Subject-specific vocabulary					
Bullet point list					

Now try this again for your least favourite subject. Are there key differences between the way you look at your favourite and least favourite subjects? For example, do you spend as much time on your least favourite subject as you do on your favourite subject?

DON'T FORGET

You need to practise these techniques for them to become an automatic part of the learning process.

THINGS TO DO AND THINK ABOUT

Start now to use at least one of the techniques from this chapter in every study session. Try to use everything from the list at some point.

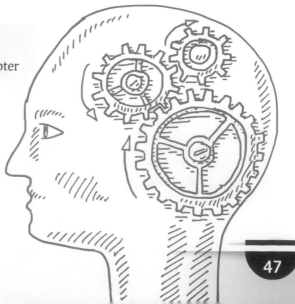

PLANNING YOUR STUDY PROGRAMME

REMEMBER – LEARNING NEW THINGS

Remember is the second stage in the **3Rs** process. In the remember stage, you have to make your short- and long-term memories hold all the information you gathered during the **review** stage. In this section, you will be looking at ways to prompt your brain to remember the keywords.

PLANNING FOR STUDY

Effective study plans will employ a range of different study skills. This is important to keep your study varied, your brain interested and to enable you to learn different types of information.

Although there are lots of different methods available for learning, it is important that you make sure you use the best methods for you. Some people can put a lot of time into their study yet not get the grades they expect. One reason for this could be that they are not effective in committing the information to their memory because they have not worked out their most effective ways of learning.

A lot of inexperienced learners simply read over their notes again and again. This may help them to remember some information, but it is not recognised as active study and may not be very effective. It may not be suitable for the person's learning style. The brain may get bored with the same method and there is no testing to check how much has been committed to memory.

You should use a study plan (see pages 32–33) as a vital tool in supporting your homework and study programme. It can be a diary or a chart on your wall or a document on your computer or phone – whatever works for you. Use it to record your homework, study, dates for assessment, test results and deadlines for handing in work.

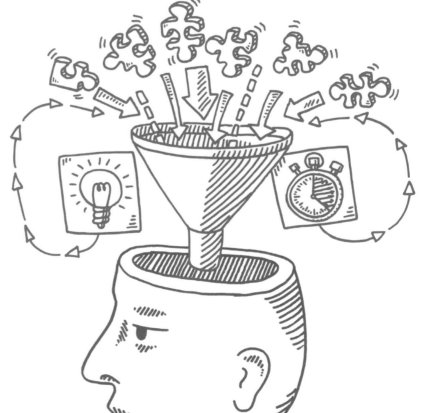

+ DON'T FORGET

The remember sections in the ideal study hour are crucial for learning information. See pages 28–31 to remind yourself how to construct an ideal study hour.

+ DON'T FORGET

When and where you study is an individual preference and will depend on the type of work you are doing. Learning new concepts might require a lot of concentration in a quiet room, but for other tasks you might prefer appropriate background music.

↑ TOP TIP

If you've completed your study charts, you will know that you have tried hard to learn the material, and this will give you the confidence to write good, detailed answers.

If you are studying for certificated subjects, you should be doing **at least one hour** of homework and study five times per week. This time includes research for portfolios and added value units. Two hours per session is the optimum time to get better results and really do yourself justice. Try to work out priorities:

- Firstly, do the **homework** given out by your teacher.
- Secondly, **revise** the work you have recently covered in class, do some general revision or research for assignments.

Record what you have done in your plan. There should be no blank sessions as you should be studying or researching if you have no homework. Aim to develop a programme to cover all your subjects.

It is important to have a flexible programme which:

- takes account of your homework, study and leisure activities
- allows you to plan your study around your homework
- gives you an overview of how much time you have given to each subject
- increases your confidence when you can see at a glance how much you have done.

QUALITY OF HOMEWORK AND STUDY

Always aim to do the best quality homework and study that you can in the allotted time. Use class notes, revision guides such as **BrightRED books** and websites such as the **BrightRED Digital Zone** or **BBC Bitesize** so you know the correct subject vocabulary to use and you know that your information is accurate.

Planning how long you think the piece of work should take you is good practice for keeping to time in your tests.

Do not spend hours struggling away on a difficult piece of work. Do what you can in a reasonable time, and then talk with your teacher later, explaining what you tried to do and how long you spent on it. To be able to do this, try to do your homework as soon as possible after you get it. This will allow you time to speak with your teacher and make changes before the piece of work is due to be handed in.

HOW YOUR HOMEWORK SUPPORTS THE REMEMBER STAGE

Homework reinforces and develops your classwork and helps you to commit it to your memory. It gives you the opportunity to:

- reflect on your classwork so your brain starts to connect and categorise the information
- commit the work covered in class to your long-term memory
- do further research on topics
- practise skills and techniques
- practise for tests
- prepare for assessments.

THINGS TO DO AND THINK ABOUT

Draw up your own study programme and follow it for one month.

TECHNIQUES FOR REINFORCING AND REMEMBERING INFORMATION 1

Study is all about trying to develop techniques to help you understand, remember and apply your knowledge. In this section, we're going to look at techniques to help you **remember** that knowledge, so it moves from your short-term to your long-term memory.

Some people take longer to learn than others. Even quick learners don't always catch on right away. Everyone can learn more effectively if they have a good set of study techniques at their disposal. You should try to use a range of techniques to make your study more fun. You should also tailor your choices to your preferred thinking and learning styles to help with the range of tasks you will be asked to do.

REVIEW: RECAP

To make your learning easier and more effective, remember to use the techniques you developed during the **review** stage:

- Shorten your class notes to the briefest possible form using keywords.
- If you're a picture person, use diagrams and patterns.
- If you're a word person, use rhymes, word pairs and mnemonics.
- Highlight keywords and important points in your notes.
- Leave study notes stuck where you will see them – by your TV or favourite poster.
- Do self-test exercises to check what you've learned or ask your study supporters to help test your memory.
- Make a note of your weak areas and target them in your study programme.
- Split your subjects into topics to make it easier to learn small sections at a time.
- Write key points on large sheets of paper and hang them on your bedroom walls – this makes them more familiar and easier to remember.

STUDY NOTES

Study notes can be in a range of formats. Try to use different methods to make your study interesting and varied so your brain doesn't get bored. You should also include marked answers or tests in your study notes. Ticks or positive comments suggest where you will gain marks, and suggested improvements are areas you need to learn and include in future answers.

You will probably see and use different formats in your own class notes and in books and handouts. In your class notes:

- highlight key words and phrases in colour
- write comments or notes in margins or spaces at the top and bottom of pages.

A shortened, concise set of notes can include key points and the things you find difficult to remember. You can make up a system to check off what you are good at remembering – ☺ or ✓ – and what you find hard to remember – ☹ or ✗.

This could even be underlining the things you remember in one colour and the things you find hard in another.

In textbooks and handouts:

- Use the 'Don't forget' sections such as this one in a physics book.
- Use the summary sections such as this one in BrightRED Study Guide N5 Mathematics.
- Write comments or notes in margins or spaces at the top and bottom of pages.
- Use online resources provided to back up the learning from your book such as this test link from BrightRED Study Guide N5 English.

DON'T FORGET

Writing your comments at the top, bottom or side of the page makes it easy to see them when you flick through the pages. You can also use them to check if you remember the key points on that page.

DON'T FORGET

Potential difference or voltage is measured in volts and 1 volt (1 V) is equivalent to 1 joule per coulomb $(1\,J\,C^{-1})$.

SUMMARY

After studying the two sections on multiplying out brackets, you should be able to:

- simplify $ax(bx + c)$
- simplify $a(bx + c) + d(ex + f)$
- simplify $(ax + b)(bx + c)$ including $(ax + b)^2$
- simplify $(ax + b)(cx^2 + dx + e)$

where a, b, c, d, e and f are integers.

ONLINE TEST

To test your overall knowledge of group discussions, take the 'Lost for words' test at www.brightredbooks.net/N5English.

THINGS TO DO AND THINK ABOUT

Whichever type of study notes you use, it can be really helpful to use different colours or symbols to highlight parts which give a really good **description** or a detailed **explanation**, or are points you might want to use if you are asked to **discuss** the topic. These are all the things which may help you to get marks for your answers.

TECHNIQUES FOR REINFORCING AND REMEMBERING INFORMATION 2

LEARNING NOTES

Study notes are a very important part of a successful study plan. However, the effects of making good notes and planning out your time will be severely limited if you don't actually learn the information.

You must make sure you tap into your own personal preferred learning styles. (Go back to pages 20–23 if you need a reminder about learning styles.) If you are an **auditory learner**, recite things either by talking them through out loud or in your mind. Using rhymes and rhythms can help. **Visual learners** should use diagrams, pictures and colour in their notes, while **kinaesthetic learners** will probably feel most comfortable writing things out several times. It has been shown that simply reading something over and over again is not the best way to remember information and should not be your main study method.

How you learn will also depend on what you are learning. For lists, mnemonics are very effective. For short answers, keywords are useful. In extended essays, mind-maps can give structure and flow by concentrating on the main strand keywords that the question focuses on and drawing in relevant information from the other strands.

KEEP ALL YOUR NOTES AND LOOK AT THEM

Never throw out any study notes you make. They can be used again after a few months to check that the information is in your long-term memory. If there is anything which you can't remember, you only have to go back and remind yourself of that small section.

Familiarise yourself with the key information or hard-to-learn facts. This will start to lodge the information in your long-term memory, ready to be used in assignments and exams. There are a lot of ways you can reinforce your learning:

- Keep all study notes and regularly look at them.
- Draw posters or key prompts lists and hang them on your bedroom wall.
- Hang mind-maps on the wall with a specific area for each subject.
- Stick post-it notes with key information around your mirror or on your wall.
- Hijack your little brother or sister's alphabet fridge magnets to help your spelling or language vocabulary learning.
- Create a special **REMEMBER** page on your computer, phone or in your notebook. Read it daily, deleting information you can now remember and adding new information to be learned. Use colour and pictures to help you remember.
- Record information using voice programmes on your computer or phone and listen to them or recite along with them.
- Make up prompt cards – get small pieces of card, write a question on one side and the answer on the other. This helps you to remember *and* apply your knowledge, particularly if you use questions from previous tests and exams.

ACTIVITY

Based on these techniques, complete the following table:

	Already use	Will now use
Keep study notes	Yes / No	Yes / No
Posters	Yes / No	Yes / No
Mind-maps	Yes / No	Yes / No
Post-its	Yes / No	Yes / No
Alphabet magnets	Yes / No	Yes / No
'Remember' computer page	Yes / No	Yes / No
Record key points	Yes / No	Yes / No

DON'T FORGET

Use the methods which best suit your personal thinking and learning styles

Remember, if you don't use any of these, don't start by trying to use them all at once. Choose two or three to start with. Once you have got into the habit of using them, then use more. If you find you don't like one method, try another. These won't all work for everyone; find which ones are best for you.

Once you have selected which methods you are going to use, get into a routine where you will spend a few minutes each day looking at your prompts. Choose the time to suit you – it could be first thing in the morning, when you return home, before you start your homework study programme, or as part of the ideal study hour.

Whatever methods you use to remember information, you must check whether you've learned it or not. The best way to do this is by using the **look/cover/write/check** method which we will look at in more detail on the next two pages.

THINGS TO DO AND THINK ABOUT

Choose one aspect of your work which you find difficult to remember such as spelling, learning new vocabulary or learning a list. Write out the list – use your phone if possible. Delete items from your list once you can remember them and replace them with new 'hard-to-learn' items.

LOOK/COVER/WRITE/CHECK

Look/cover/write/check is a methodical, four-stage process that will help you move information from your short-term to your long-term memory.

STAGE 1: LOOK

This involves looking over and trying to internalise the information you want to learn. You might recite it over and over, use a mnemonic or write it out several times. (Whatever technique you choose, it should reflect your preferred learning style.)

The aim is to help the brain to make connections with the information and become familiar with it. Focusing on keywords, subject-specific vocabulary and key concepts will help the brain to make connections with previous experience and banks of information. This is the start of the process which commits the information to memory.

If you are trying to remember a long piece of work, pick out the keyword or theme of each paragraph and learn this in the correct order. Remember, mnemonics will help you with this.

STAGE 2: COVER

Cover up your work so you can't see it. Not even a peek!

STAGE 3: WRITE

You can do this in different ways. One of the best ways is to write out what you have tried to learn in Stage 1, because it is easy for you to see whether you've remembered it or not.

You could recite the information to yourself or recite it to a parent, guardian or friend. If you are learning vocabulary –particularly for a foreign language – you need to **say** the words too, so that you work on the correct pronunciation and get used to hearing yourself say them.

Whatever technique you choose, use the keywords, subject-specific vocabulary and key concepts as the triggers and prompts to help your brain to remember banks of related information.

The keywords you learned, in order, from each paragraph can help you with the content and structure for extended pieces of writing **and** oral assessments.

STAGE 4: CHECK

TOP TIP

You can often learn more from a wrong answer – it might be that you don't fully understand the concept or that there is a gap in your knowledge.

This stage is very important. Check your Stage 3 answer to find out what you have got correct, what you missed out and what you got wrong.

It is sometimes only when you check your answer that you become aware that it doesn't read well, it doesn't flow, bits are missing or there are things that you don't understand clearly. You could also compare the quality of your answer with your notes, model answers or past paper answers.

Note any errors, gaps or areas where you need to add more detail. (Remember – mnemonics help you to remember lists.) Perhaps you will have to go back to your notes or books, do further research or ask your teacher to help you to fill in these gaps.

Don't be afraid to ask your teacher for help. If you have tried to improve a piece of work and you feel that it's still not as good as it could be, or if you still don't understand what's involved, discuss it with your teacher.

If it's not possible to speak with your teacher before, during or after the lesson, then ask if you can have a few minutes of their time at interval, lunchtime or after school.

Once you are confident that you have relearned what you forgot, filled in the gaps or have a better understanding of the information, check again in a few days' time to see if you remember it. If you still find it difficult to remember, keep repeating the process until the information becomes familiar, then 'check' again.

TRY DIFFERENT METHODS

Keep using the **look/cover/write/check** process, but don't be too hard on yourself with the things you find difficult to learn. You will naturally remember some things more easily than others.

If it is really hard for you to remember a particular piece of work, try changing the method you are using to learn it. For example, if you make a mnemonic and you still can't remember what it means, try drawing a diagram of the topic, make up a 'hard-to-learn' poster or put the information in a table or graph format. You could hang your diagram, poster, table or graph on your wall or stick it next to the mirror. Or you could put it into a document on your computer desktop or set it up as a background so you could quickly look at it every time you open up your computer. You could even send it to your phone.

THINGS TO DO AND THINK ABOUT

Remember to record the things that you can't remember or get wrong and check them regularly until they become more familiar to your brain.

Sometimes you can replace the look/cover process with reflective thinking. Without looking at your notes can you try to remember the keywords and related banks of information?

When you can do this, your brain is getting really good at recalling these familiar keywords and connecting them to the relevant information. This means that you are entering the autonomous stage for remembering this information. In other words, you will eventually remember this information easily and quickly, without having to think about it too much. Then you can try to add more information to give greater depth and detail.

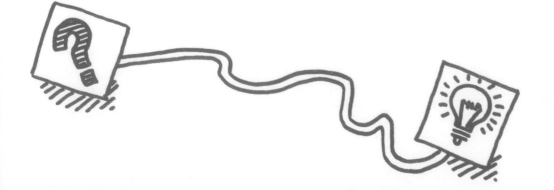

TOP TIP

Study clubs can give you the opportunity to speak to your teacher about any worries you have. It's highly likely that if you are having problems, then your peers will be having them, too.

STUDY SUPPORT

Use the look/cover/write/check method during your next three study sessions. Ask you helpers to support you. They can make learning more fun and help to motivate you and build your confidence.

DON'T FORGET

Highlight things that you can't remember and prioritise them until they are lodged in your memory.

6 RECALL

TECHNIQUES FOR RECALLING WHAT YOU HAVE LEARNED 1

Recall is the third stage in the **3Rs process**. This chapter explores the ways in which the prompts and information learned in the previous two stages are recalled and developed into detailed answers.

APPLYING WHAT YOU HAVE LEARNED

In the context of study techniques, recall is more than just quickly remembering the information you have learned. It is about **applying** what you have learned to give the correct and appropriate response to specific exam and assessment questions. This involves:

- interpreting and understanding questions so you know what is being asked
- recalling relevant knowledge and using prompts to help structure answers
- developing assessment techniques (such as using layout and understanding timing) so that you can write a fluent answer in the time available.

In short, your brain processes all the prompts and information you have learned and uses these to build up your answers. But first of all, we'll look at how you can recall the information you have learned.

PROMPTS

The short, brief prompts – such as mnemonics, diagrams and rhymes – that you used in your study notes should stimulate your brain to make the connections to recall a bank of knowledge. You should be able to expand on these few words or diagrams to help you construct an in-depth and detailed answer.

Here is an example of how to use a **mnemonic** and a bit of general knowledge to build up an answer to the following question:

EXAMPLE

Discuss 'what is a rainbow?'

For this question, you would remember the mnemonic ROY G BIV or **R**ichard **O**f **Y**ork **G**ave **B**attle **I**n **V**ain, which gives the order of the colours that light is split into when the sun shines through rain. You could answer the question like this:

A rainbow is an arc of coloured light which sweeps up to the sky from the ground. As the sun shines through rain, light is broken into the colours of the spectrum. These are red, orange, yellow, green, blue, indigo and violet. They always appear in the same order. Some people like to tell the old wives' tale that says 'there is a pot of gold at the end of every rainbow', but none has ever been found. Some scientists have questioned whether indigo actually exists as they consider it to be within the violet section. Although there is much discussion, it hasn't yet been excluded.

You can use a similar process to form an answer from the key points in your books or study notes. For example, let's explore a question taken from the SQA *N5 Business Management Specimen Question Paper*:

> 4 (b) Outline 3 factors an organisation would consider when
> choosing a supplier.   **3 marks**

To answer this question you could research the relevant section in *BrightRED Study Guide N5 Business Management* and identify the key points.

SELECTING A SUPPLIER OF RAW MATERIALS

When choosing a supplier of raw materials, the operations department needs to take the following factors into account.

Quality
Is the quality of the raw materials on offer of a satisfactory standard?

Time
Potential suppliers of raw materials should be able to deliver by the date requested.

Quantity
Any potential supplier of raw materials must be able to meet the quantities required by the operations department.

Price
The lowest price for the quality desired should be sought to ensure value for money. Discounts should be requested for good custom and bulk buying.

Dependability
Potential suppliers must be dependable, respectable, likely to stay in business and have reliable delivery systems in place.

Location
If the supplier is not close by, there could be expensive delivery charges.

Using the sections highlighted in the extract above, you might come up with an answer like:

*An organisation would check that the **quality** of the supplier's materials was of a high enough standard, that its materials could be delivered on **time** and that it could supply adequate **quantities** to meet operational demands.*

THINGS TO DO AND THINK ABOUT

1. Use one of your own mnemonics (from the activity on page 41) to build up an answer.

2. Build up an answer from keywords and key points in your study notes. If possible, use a question from your homework or a past exam paper.

TECHNIQUES FOR RECALLING WHAT YOU HAVE LEARNED 2

DIAGRAMS AND GRAPHS

Diagrams and graphs can be extremely useful for summarising and recalling a lot of data. They also help to structure answers, as referring to the diagram helps to ensure that everything is mentioned and prompts the order of the topics.

Diagrams and graphs can be used in a number of ways:

- They can be learned and drawn in assessments to give a lot of information clearly and quickly. Diagrams and graphs in portfolios, essays and exam answers must be fully labelled.
- Labels provide prompts, ensuring that all the relevant information is included. This will help to add depth to answers and potentially gain more marks.
- Good diagrams and graphs help to show understanding of the concept or topic.

EXAMPLE

This example from *BrightRED Study Guide N5 Geography* clearly shows how useful a diagram is for answering a question.

This question is taken from the SQA *N5 Geography Specimen Question Paper*:

Question 2 - rivers and valleys

(a)   Study OS map Item A of the Dingwall area. Use the information in the OS map Item A to match the features of rivers and valleys in the table below with the correct grid reference.

Features of rivers and valleys:

v-shaped valley, meander, river flowing NW

Choose from grid references:

522623   457668   523594   435663

Use the information from the diagram and 2nd, 4th and 6th bullet points.

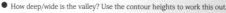

RIVERS

When describing a river on an O.S. map it is important to look at the *physical* (natural) features of the river and its valley. Ask yourself these questions about the river:

- Is the river in its **upper**, **middle** or **lower course**?
- What is the shape of the valley? Lots of contours suggest a **steep V-shaped valley**; few contours may suggest a **gently sloping valley** in the lower course.
- Is there land on either side without contours? If so, may be a **flood plain**.
- Can you identify river landforms (e.g. **meanders**, **ox-bow lakes**, **tributaries**, etc.) with six-figure grid references?
- What is the **name** of the river and the names of any tributaries?
- In which **direction** does the river flow?
- How deep/wide is the valley? Use the contour heights to work this out.

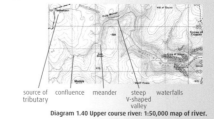

source of   confluence   meander   steep   waterfalls
tributary   V-shaped
                                        valley

Diagram 1.40 Upper course river: 1:50,000 map of river.

DON'T FORGET ✚

You can check your knowledge using online tests at www.brightredbooks.net

ACTIVITY

Use the **look/cover/draw/check** technique to learn the diagram and labels below, then answer the questions that follow. The bullet points at the side have been added to give more information, and are particularly useful if you are not a biology student.

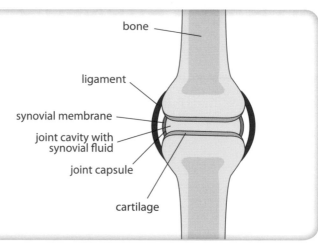

Synovial joint

- Cartilage is smooth to reduce friction.
- Cartilage is spongy to absorb shocks.
- Synovial fluid is produced by the synovial membrane – reduces friction in the joint.
- Bones are held together by elastic ligaments.
- Hinge joint:
  - found at the elbow, knee and fingers.
  - permits movement in a single plane of movement (bend and straighten).

bone

ligament

synovial membrane

joint cavity with synovial fluid

joint capsule

cartilage

1. Use the following questions to evaluate yourself:

   Did you remember most of the labels?   *Yes/NO*

   Did you remember most of the picture?   *Yes/NO*

   Did this method work for you?   *Yes/NO*

   Has the diagram helped you to remember the information?   *Yes/NO*

2. Use the labels in the diagram – ligament, synovial membrane, joint cavity with synovial fluid, joint capsule, bone, cartilage – to answer this question:

   > Describe a synovial joint.

   If you are a biology student, try to do this by remembering the bullet point information. If you are not a biology student, you can look at the above bullet points to help you create your answer.

3. Try the look/cover/draw/check technique again, this time using a diagram from your own notes. List the bullet points that might be needed in an answer.

DON'T FORGET

Labelling diagrams helps to show your depth of knowledge and the labels are key words to help you recall background information.

THINGS TO DO AND THINK ABOUT

This process of learning from and drawing diagrams and graphs is particularly useful to visual learners. However, some answers, particularly in the sciences, will require diagrams. It is therefore important that all types of learner should be able to use this technique. It can also save time in an exam because diagrams require less writing.

Kinaesthetic learners could also benefit from imagining a diagram in their heads, then going through each part of it systematically and imagining what each part of the joint does when it is being used. This could result in the following answer:

1. Types of joint – hinge, ball and socket
2. Bones – held together by ligaments
3. Synovial membrane – synovial fluid, reduces friction
4. Cartilage – smooth, spongy

As most people use more than one learning style, **visual** and **auditory** learners could also use parts of this process.

TECHNIQUES FOR RECALLING WHAT YOU HAVE LEARNED 3

MIND-MAPS

Mind-maps are not only really useful when you are trying to learn information which you will **remember** in exams – they can also help to structure answers.

In most exams, the examiners will use certain key concepts when making up the questions to prompt the answers they want. If your strands correspond to the key concepts then you should have the main points required for answering the question. In extended answers, the main focus of a question may be on one strand. The details on this strand would form the basis and main focus of the answer, but related topics from other strands could give added depth to the answer, scoring more points.

This example from Physical Education contains no illustrations so it could be called a **text map**. It shows how using concepts in different strands can enhance an answer.

EXAMPLE

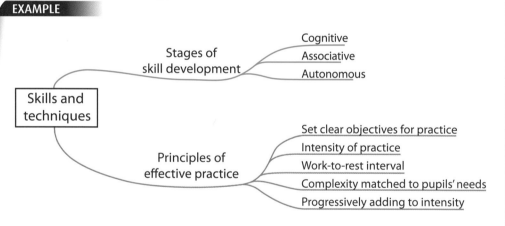

Skills and techniques

Stages of skill development
- Cognitive
- Associative
- Autonomous

Principles of effective practice
- Set clear objectives for practice
- Intensity of practice
- Work-to-rest interval
- Complexity matched to pupils' needs
- Progressively adding to intensity

A mind-map or text map like this could be used to help answer a question such as this:

Question 5

When learning and developing a skill, it is important to work through the three stages of learning.

These are:

- the learning/cognitive stage
- the practice/associative stage
- the automatic/autonomous stage.

Choose an activity and a skill or technique.

(d) Justify the course of action you took to improve your performance. **6**

Before answering, you need to read the question carefully and identify that the different parts of the question are asking about different concepts. The key concept the examiners are asking about is **principles of effective practice**. The answer should therefore include all the information on the principles of effective practice strand of the mind-map. The answer would link the principles of effective practice to the stages of skill development outlined at the start of the question.

*Setting clear objectives meant focusing on my main weakness throughout all my programme. My practices in **each of the stages** were chosen to develop this weakness...*

or

*As my weakness improved, I made the practices **progressively more intensive** by increasing the amount of time spent on each practice and the difficulty of the practice. Practices in the **cognitive stage** were simple, becoming more complex and intense as I worked through the **associative** and **autonomous** stages...*

Look at the words in bold and work out the strands they appear in.

The mind-map helped the learner to ensure that the **main** focus was on the **principles** strand and, although mentioning **stages of learning**, it didn't let the answer drift into the other strand in too much depth. This is important under exam conditions when time for planning and rearranging work is limited.

Mind-maps can also be very useful in self-evaluation. See page 70.

PAST PAPERS

Past papers from previous exams are available on the SQA's website. The past papers are provided with marking schemes, which are really useful for guiding you towards what will actually gain you marks in your answers.

Past papers, sample answers and marking schemes are used extensively prior to exams as they:

- demonstrate the level and style or layout of the exam
- let pupils practise using realistic questions
- have clear time limits so pupils can practise answering the questions in the time allowed
- allow pupils to compare their answers to sample answers and marking schemes
- help pupils to understand exactly what the question is asking and what the marker expects.

DON'T FORGET

Use subject-specific vocabulary and add definitions to give strong, detailed answers in exams and assignments.

THINGS TO DO AND THINK ABOUT

Use your mind-maps, keywords and headings in your notes to help you plan and structure your answer so it flows in a logical order. Compare your answers to model and past paper answers.

APPLYING WHAT YOU HAVE LEARNED

Now that you are able to recall or access the information stored in your brain, it's time to apply it in a range of contexts.

APPLY HIGHER ORDER THINKING SKILLS

You looked briefly at Bloom's Revised Taxonomy triangle earlier on in the guide. To remind yourself of this, go back to p11 and have a look at the diagram below. In your exams and assignments for National 4, National 5 and Higher, you will be expected to apply these higher order thinking skills up to the 'evaluating' level (that is, remembering, understanding, applying, analysing, and evaluating).

Higher Order Thinking Skills

Level	I can use information to:
Creating	build new ideas
Evaluating	express and back up my opinions
Analysing	by breaking it down to understand better
Applying	in a new way
Understanding	to explain ideas
Remembering	to remember

Lower Order Thinking Skills

Try to practise using and developing these thinking skills in class or when you are doing your homework. Once you've got some experience under your belt, you can start to use higher order thinking skills when you are studying, so you will be able to apply your knowledge to new questions or to anticipate exam questions.

Asking Thinking Questions

I can use information to:

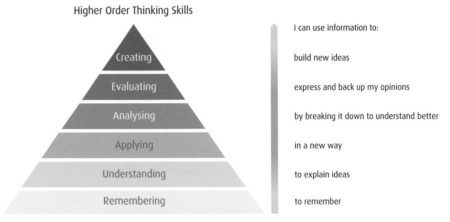

I can use information to:	Asking Thinking Questions
to build new ideas	Creating: How could you improve/develop? What might be a solution to...?
to express and back up my opinion	Evaluating: What shows that? What evidence supports your view?
by breaking it down to understand it better	Analysing: What is similar or different to? Is the information based on fact or opinion?
in a new way	Applying: How would you solve? What can you use to explain...?
to explain ideas	Understanding: How would you explain? Tell me in your own words...
to remember facts	Remember: What is? What happened after...?

To develop thinking skills, you need to ask thinking questions such as 'How can I solve?' or 'What evidence do I have?' You will find that these 'thinking questions' will be really useful when you are researching and doing portfolios and added value units where you are not asked many direct questions. You might have to look at research to find evidence to support your view or back up your findings in an experiment.

PROBLEM-SOLVING

The higher order thinking questions are at the heart of problem-solving. Remember to ask yourself 'What do I know?' to help you to access the information you have learned. Asking questions such as 'What do I want to find out...?', 'What are the links between...?' or 'How can this relate to...?' will help you to make the connections that will bring about solutions.

USING THE INTERNET FOR STUDY SUPPORT

Many websites not only have reliable information – they are also stimulating and will motivate and inspire you to study. Interactive learning is particularly good for **kinaesthetic learners**. The visuals and videos on the sites will appeal to **visual learners**. Videos, readings, and voice-overs are good for **auditory learners** to listen to. The range and variety of exercises will appeal to **most** learners. Here are some examples:

- Some websites contain materials for specific courses – for example, the **BrightRED Digital Zone** (www.brightredbooks.net) and **BBC Bitesize** (www.bbc.co.uk/education) both cater for SQA courses.

- National 5 and CfE Higher *BrightRED Study Guides* contain links that will take you online to further information, suggested answers or tests on the specific topic you have been working on.

- Many websites are interactive and contain quizzes and games that test how much you have learned.

- You can practise your maths skills on some websites by competing against people from around the world.

- Some websites have discussion rooms where you can ask questions and develop ideas with other students.

Ask your teachers or tutors to recommend good quality websites that relate to your course.

Many schools and colleges have their own Virtual Learning Environments (VLEs), with material and exercises for specific courses uploaded by staff to support their learners.

Education Scotland's website hosts 'Glow' – the world's first national online community for education at http://www.educationscotland.gov.uk/usingglowandict/. It gives information about games-based learning and how pupils and educators can log in to access the huge bank of resources for 3 to 18 year-olds.

THINGS TO DO AND THINK ABOUT

Using the internet to test your learning can be quick and fun. However, remember that you will have to write your responses in timed assessments, so practise this in your study.

PLANNING ESSAYS AND EXTENDED ANSWERS

Essays and extended answers require more forward planning than short answers. You should always try to create a **structure** which makes the answer flow, rather than jump from one topic to another and back again.

CREATING A STRUCTURE FOR YOUR ESSAYS

Essays need to have some kind of logical structure for them to gain maximum marks. Most essays will use the following structure:

- Start with the **introduction**. This introduces the topic, sets the scene, introduces characters or gives definitions in more fact-based subjects such as the sciences.
- Each paragraph should deal with a **separate topic**.
- The paragraphs should be in a **logical order** to develop the topic, theme or storyline.
- If the question asks you to discuss a topic, make sure you give **alternative points of view** or **options.**
- Finish with a **conclusion**. This should be **concise** and **clear**, mentioning key points, and should flow logically from the points made in the body of the essay.

CREATIVE WRITING

Creative writing can be more complicated, and a storyboard can help you to plan the different elements. You could include the following:

- an introduction that grabs the reader's attention
- clear character descriptions
- a plan that makes it clear when you're going to introduce characters
- a vivid description of the scene/context within which the story is set
- summary of the main storyline
- summary of secondary storylines
- a timeline that links the storyline with characters, scene changes, and so on
- an impactful ending.

The storyboard can be in a variety of forms. You could, for example, subdivide it into scenes, as follows:

EXAMPLE

1 Murder scene set

2 Key characters introduced

3 Love interest introduced – hinders investigation

4 Conflict between characters

5 New lead followed up

6 Surprise killer uncovered

Another way of developing the storyboard would be to use brief notes or even drawings of stick men.

DISCURSIVE WRITING

In English, you will cover a range of writing skills, including discursive writing. This can either be **argumentative** – where you put forward different points of view or **persuasive** –where you try to win over the reader. The *BrightRED Study Guide N5 English* gives you the key points about this type of writing, along with online support and tests.

Scene setting	Victim: Murdered by single blow to the head No weapon Industrial estate Time of death 8–9pm No witnesses, no CCTV Male (in his 30s) from nearby estate, no previous record, cocaine in pocket – drugs deal?
Key characters	Detective team: DI, handsome, good at his job Superintendent, pressurises, unrealistic DC in awe of DI
Conflicts/love interest	Few leads – interviews families and local workers Victim's sister adamant victim did not take drugs DI looks for non-drugs lead – others in team think he's influenced by sister – potential relationship Victim's bank records show large withdrawal
New evidence	Industrial estate searched again – large wrench found with blood on it among industrial rubbish DNA taken from wrench DNA match from security guard at nearby factory
Solution and conclusion	Motive discovered – con trick – victim buying a car, not up to standard, doesn't want to buy it, murderer threatens, fight, and didn't mean to kill Security guard arrested DI meets sister for dinner ...

EXTENDED ANSWER STRUCTURE

The writing skills that you are taught in English can be used across the curriculum in your other subjects. The same basic structure applies:

- Start with the **introduction**.
- Each paragraph should deal with a **separate topic**.
- The paragraphs should be in a **logical order** to develop the topic or theme.
- If the question asks you to discuss a topic, make sure you give **alternative points of view** or **options**.
- Finish with a **conclusion**. This should be **concise** and **clear**, mentioning key points, and should flow logically from the points made in the body of the essay.

This structure can be applied to extended answers and to short and long essays. It can be used at all levels from National 4 to Advanced Higher, in portfolios, added value units, research assignments and exams.

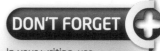

DON'T FORGET

In your writing, use **subject-specific** vocabulary whenever you can.

THINGS TO DO AND THINK ABOUT

When you are writing, try to include your keywords/subject-specific vocabulary with definitions to add more depth and detail to your writing.

RESEARCH

Many courses will include a **research task** as part of the ongoing assessment. The topic chosen for the research task will usually build on work done in the classroom. Before starting your research, select the keywords that will help you to focus on the specific type of information you need for your answer. Sometimes the marking scheme will be available for you to look at. If this is the case, read it, take note of the **key features** and **key concepts** and build your research around these points. Marking schemes are available on the SQA website.

There are two main ways of finding information:

- **literature search** – looking for information in books, journals, newspapers and other printed material
- **internet search** – using the internet to access information from sources worldwide.

LITERATURE SEARCH

A literature search involves using books, journals, newspapers and other printed materials. Some courses will issue lists of books that contain the most relevant information. If you don't have a book list, ask your teacher or tutor if there are any particularly good books that would help you.

Newspapers can be very good for charting the development of an event or new initiative. Check which newspapers are available in your school Library Resource Centre – you could use these in your research. Back copies or older issues of newspapers can be accessed in some local libraries or at the newspapers' offices. Perhaps the easiest way of accessing back copies is by looking in the archive section of the newspaper's website.

If you are using a newspaper article in your research, however, you should always bear in mind that it is a subjective account, based on the individual views and opinions of the reporter (and, sometimes, of the newspaper). Different newspapers will probably report the same event or story quite differently.

If there's a particularly useful book in the library that a number of people want to use at the same time, you will probably have to access it in the reference section. Important books are kept in this section for people to use, but you can't take them home. You might, therefore, have to allow time for this and start to plan your research early, so you don't leave it to the last minute.

Some libraries can arrange for you to take an extended loan, where (depending on the availability of the book) you can keep it for a longer period of time. Many college and university libraries will also offer an online service for reserving books or extending your loan period. This can save you time going backwards and forwards to the library.

INTERNET SEARCH

Over the last few years, the internet has become an invaluable source of easy-to-access information. Using keywords in search engines generally brings up a lot of information. But be careful about the keywords you use – too few words could give you too many (mostly irrelevant) results but too many specific words could limit your search and result in you missing out on some good material.

Entering an author's name in a browser will often bring up other people's analyses of their stories or poems. These can be really helpful, because while they will flag up some of the key ideas that you already know about, they will probably also flag up some that you don't know about or hadn't thought of, and these could help you score extra marks.

Use sites such as Wikipedia with great care. The information in Wikipedia can be edited by anyone and so some of it might not be true. However, it does contain many links to high quality, reputable sites that can help you to validate the information and even find out more.

IDENTIFYING RELEVANT AND RELIABLE INFORMATION QUICKLY

Whatever your method of accessing information, here are a few tips to help you to work out quickly whether or not a particular source has relevant and reliable information:

- Look at the contents page to see if any chapters cover your area of interest.
- The start of a chapter or article will often give an outline of what it contains. If it looks like this might be helpful, flick through or read that particular chapter.
- The end of a chapter or article often contains a very useful summary of the key points. This can sometimes save you reading the whole thing.
- When you are flicking through a chapter or article, look out for the keywords that link into your area of study. If you are lucky, they might appear as subheadings or be highlighted or underlined. If you are online, type in keywords and see if they appear in the articles.
- Diagrams, tables and graphs can let you see at a glance if they are dealing with the information you want.
- Highlighted or shaded sections often contain key information. Some textbooks use highlighting and shading to summarise key information and processes.

PEER RESEARCH

If you are working as part of a group on the same topic, it's a good idea to share the research. Split the book list up between the members of the group. Each person should take brief notes on their books and highlight the really good sources that everyone else could benefit from reading.

Photocopy a copy of the notes for everyone in the group. Arrange a group meeting where everyone brings their notes and discusses the research they have investigated. This is a great time to pick up on new ideas and different interpretations.

THINGS TO DO AND THINK ABOUT

Try to use your research to get more information about your topic, seek other views or get quotes to justify your own findings.

DON'T FORGET

In your notes, always record where you get the information.

STUDY SUPPORT

Involve your helpers. If you have a long book list, it can be really helpful to get together with others to cut down the work.

DON'T FORGET

Look out for clues about what information the text contains: indexes, contents pages, headings, highlighted sections and keywords are useful for this.

HOW TO USE QUOTES, REFERENCES AND AVOID PLAGIARISM

Using quotes from books and other sources is a good way to demonstrate that you are familiar with a subject. **However, you cannot simply copy text straight out of a book or copy and paste from the internet**. This is called **plagiarism**, and if you are caught using plagiarised material in essays and exams, you will be awarded **zero marks**.

Whenever you use somebody else's work directly, you must acknowledge it or else rewrite it into your own words.

QUOTES

If you want to use somebody's exact words, you need to put them into quotation marks 'like this'.

EXAMPLE

For example, you might want to use a quote to back up your opinion:

In his book, Social Awareness, Paul Smith said: `The census showed higher levels of ill health in people from socially deprived areas'. This shows the effects that low income has on health issues.

Quotes can be very effective in showing the importance of your opinions or in developing a discussion point by highlighting the views and opinions of other writers and researchers.

ACKNOWLEDGING AN AUTHOR

EXAMPLE

If you want to use somebody's idea but don't want to quote it word for word, you can simply write:

In his book, Social Awareness, Paul Smith noted that the census showed people from socially deprived areas had higher levels of ill health than those from more affluent areas. This reinforces the relationship between income and health.

REFERENCING AND BIBLIOGRAPHY

When you are writing your work and you use material from other sources such as books or the internet, you must give appropriate **references**. These references are collated into the **bibliography**, which should appear at the end of your work. The bibliography contains all the details of books and other sources you have used. So whenever you use a source for information, note it in the bibliography straight away. Each entry has to be written in a particular way. There are different methods of referencing. Here is an example of how referencing can be done:

Author's surname, initials, date of publication, title (*in italics*), publisher, place of publication and page number(s) if appropriate.

EXAMPLE

Smith. A.S., 2009, *How to Pass Exams*, Wood Publications, London, p76.

Internet references should have the name of the author(s), title (*in italics*), website address and the date you accessed the information.

DON'T FORGET

The *name of the publication* is always written in *italics*.

EXAMPLE

Buchanan, R., *What the Queen Wears*, www.timesonline.co.uk, accessed 26/07/09.

USING YOUR OWN WORDS

You have to be very careful that you don't unwittingly use someone else's words. Use the following method to help you avoid this:

- Write down the keywords for the article.
- Cover up the article.
- Use your **reflective thinking** techniques to think about the article and build up what you want to say.
- Write out your response.
- Check that the wording of what you have written is different to that of the author.

While you are **planning** what you are going to write, try to link it into other relevant bits of information you have. Think back to your mind-maps to see if you can link in with other strands, or think of possible links with other topics, headings or keywords in your notes. Some assessments will be across various topics, so being able to find the connections between topics is a really useful skill to develop.

USING RESEARCH IN YOUR WORK

As you work through the research information you should be asking yourself:

- How can I use this information?
- Does it give my work more depth and detail?
- Does it provide evidence to support my findings?
- Does it throw up an alternative view?
- Can I use it in a different context?
- Can I adapt it to suit my needs?
- Are there parts I could quote to explain or highlight points?

You are now using the higher order thinking skills to develop your responses and answers.

DON'T FORGET

Make sure that you take a note of where you found the information – including the page number or section – as you go. It wastes a lot of time later on if you have to search for the source of your information or quote.

THINGS TO DO AND THINK ABOUT

Check if your school or college has a referencing policy, because it might vary from the one outlined above, and you should go by their guidelines.

SELF-ASSESSMENT AND CORRECTING WORK

Many people find it hard to work out how to improve a piece of work. Think about it – how often do **you** look at the mark of an assignment that you've been handed back and then just put it away, rather than noting what you've done well and what you can improve upon?

To improve your work, you need to receive **feedback** so you can evaluate your strengths and weaknesses.

FEEDBACK ON YOUR WORK

You can get feedback by:

- reading **written comments** on your work from your teacher or tutor
- **discussing** the work in class
- **comparing** your answer to a sample good answer or a marking scheme
- **working with a partner** or group to see who had the **best answer**.

IMPROVING YOUR WORK

When you are redrafting or improving marked work, you should:

- identify the bits you did well
- identify the bits you need to improve.

Using **colours and symbols** in your work will help you to identify the stronger parts of your work, which you can include in future answers, and the weaker parts or gaps, which need further development. This will make it easier for you to analyse what to put in your answer to score good marks. You should devise your own codes for this but they could be along the lines of:

✓	= good idea
*	= good point
!	= great phrase
?	= need to learn this
↔	= expand this point
X	= wrong information
V+	= use the subject-specific vocabulary/terminology

EVALUATING THE QUALITY OF THE ANSWER – THE COLOUR/SYMBOL METHOD

Just because you've written a lot doesn't mean that it is a good answer. One of the best ways to check the quality of an answer is to do a check to find out how many of the key concepts and keywords are in it.

To do this, choose a different symbol or colour for each key concept or feature. Go through your answer either highlighting or underlining, or drawing the appropriate symbol each time a key concept or keyword arises. If it could be improved upon – for example, by including more subject-specific vocabulary – then put a **V+** beside it. Make up your own symbols and colours for this.

Once you have coded your work, you should be able to analyse your strengths and weaknesses. Is one colour appearing too often? This might mean that you have spent too much time on this concept at the expense of others. Is there a colour or symbol missing completely? Perhaps it wasn't required in this answer or you might have forgotten to include it. If you have any **V+** or other symbols, then write out an improved version. The **V+** and other symbols, are really important because they can indicate where you need to change the depth or detail of your answer.

ACTIVITY

Take a piece of work that has already been marked; one that you can improve upon. Use the colour/symbol method to evaluate it. Rewrite it and ask your teacher to mark it again, letting them know how you have tried to improve it.

USING COLOUR CODING IN MIND-MAPS

If you have used a mind-map or text map to help you develop an answer, you can use the **colour coding** within it to highlight different concepts. Give each concept or strand a different colour/symbol. Now go through your answer applying these colours/symbols. Have you got a well-balanced answer, covering all the relevant concepts? Or have you spent too much time on one concept and not enough on others? Think of your answer as a big jigsaw, where you are trying to get all the relevant mind-map information into the answer at some point.

Use your higher order thinking skills to select which information you should include from your mind-map. There is no point in writing lots if it is not relevant!

You should also analyse how well you have structured your answer, and how smoothly it flows. If, for example, you are writing an extended answer you will be expected to develop one point so that it leads onto the next. Your colours or symbols should flag up if you have done this, because there will be concentrations of certain colours/symbols throughout your answer.

During all of these exercises, use your notes to ensure that you have the best information for your answers. Check what the key concepts or keywords are. If you don't know them, ask your teacher or tutor or check on the SQA website.

USING STUDY BOOKS

Study books can give useful advice for developing good answers and can reassure you that you are using the correct subject-specific vocabulary, as in the example on the right.

If you are struggling for time in an exam, this type of question can be a gift: you can answer several questions like this quickly to pick up a reasonable amount of marks.

DON'T FORGET

Use the extended answer structure on p65 to help with the flow and logical structure of your work.

EXAMPLE

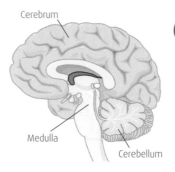

Cerebrum

Medulla

Cerebellum

DON'T FORGET

The brain and the spinal cord make up the CNS (central nervous system). The brain is composed of many different areas and each area is responsible for a different function. The three main areas are the cerebrum, cerebellum and medulla.

This diagram and 'Don't Forget' feature from the *BrightRED Study Guide N5 Biology* would help you to answer the following question from the 2014 N5 Biology exam.

5. The diagram below represents the human brain.

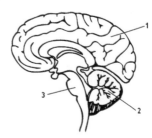

Which line in the table below identifies structures 1, 2 and 3 of the human brain?

	Structure 1	Structure 2	Structure 3
A	medulla	cerebrum	cerebellum
B	cerebrum	medulla	cerebellum
C	cerebellum	cerebrum	medulla
D	cerebrum	cerebellum	medulla

THINGS TO DO AND THINK ABOUT

STUDY SUPPORT

Involve your helpers.

Select a past paper question that has allocated more than five marks for an answer. Work out a brief plan for your answer. Use the colour/symbol technique on your plan. Does it include the appropriate symbols/colours? Now write your answer.

When you have finished writing your answer, use the colour/symbol method again. Which of the following applied to your answer?

I have included all the key concepts/words appropriately.	Yes/No
I have included most of the key concepts/words appropriately.	Yes/No
I have included some of the key concepts/words.	Yes/No
I have included a few of the key concepts/words.	Yes/No

Briefly, write what you need to do to improve your answer.

Now answer another past paper question (again, on your own). Use colour and symbols on your work to identify the good bits and the poorer parts. Get together with others and, as a group, look at everyone's answers and use them to produce what you think is a great answer.

GETTING READY FOR EXAMS

Now that you have gone through the **3Rs** process and know the material in depth, we'll look in this chapter at some of the other techniques that you can use to boost your results.

⊕ DON'T FORGET

All the assessments that you do are exams in one form or another – for example:
- portfolios
- added value units
- speaking and listening tests
- exams

SUPPORT

Remember – there are lots of people who want you to do well in your exams and who can help you with your studying.

In school, you can get support from teachers and tutors, and from other students.

Out of school, you can get support from friends and family. Being able to discuss and work through issues with your friends in the more relaxed atmosphere of each other's houses can make learning more effective and fun. When they see you working with friends in this way, parents and guardians will understand the effort you are putting in and will want to get involved to help you.

STUDY SUPPORT

Involve your helpers.

STUDY BUDDIES AND STUDY GROUPS

If your school or college offers study groups, take advantage of them. They are a really good way of getting to meet like-minded people and learning more about your subjects at the same time.

Alternatively, you might prefer to work with one other person or a small group of friends. Go with whatever works for you.

Working with a study buddy and/or study group means that you can:

- **Encourage** each other to study even when you're not in the mood. Studying with friends makes learning more fun. (Just be careful that you spend your time studying, not chatting.)

- **Share note-taking and research**. If you have a long reading list or a lot of websites to search, split the research between you. Photocopy your notes for your buddy or group. Discuss these within the group to get the full context and depth of information for your answer. In some cases, you might just need the odd quote from the notes, but you won't need to read through them all yourself. This will leave you more time for writing your assignment. (Remember – always note the source of your information for your references and bibliography.)

- **Develop new ideas** by discussing work with your group or study buddy – they might have different ideas or ways of approaching an answer that you could use.

- **Develop a deeper understanding** of the course materials by discussing and exploring them with your group or study buddy.

PARENTS, GUARDIANS, FAMILY AND FRIENDS

Parents, guardians, family and friends can all be really useful in supporting your learning, even if they don't know or understand the materials.

For example, during **look/cover/write/check**, give your notes or book to your helper and instead of writing notes down yourself, explain to them what you are trying to learn. They can check whether you've got it right. This can be more fun than trying to do it all on your own. It will also help them to understand how hard you are working.

You could also ask them to read over your work for spelling and grammar errors. Often it is very difficult for us to check our own work as our brain reads what we meant to write and so misses errors. Professional writers always employ someone to proofread their work for errors.

DON'T FORGET ⊕

If possible, ask someone to read over your drafts, re-drafts and final submissions for portfolios and added value units.

SCHOOL STUDY CLUBS, TEACHERS AND TUTORS

Most schools set up study support sessions including Easter study clubs, lunchtime study sessions or after-school sessions with a teacher. You might also be able to arrange to study individually or as part of a small group with your teacher. Your parents might arrange for you to go to a tutor or for a tutor to come to your house.

If any of these options are available to you, then make the most of them: it is amazing what you can get through during these sessions. The work tends to be very focused on your needs and on the exam. Even pieces of work that you've struggled to understand can become much clearer as the teacher or tutor addresses your specific strengths and weaknesses.

USE YOUR STUDY NOTES

Once you've made notes during your study time, **never** throw them away. Use them later to check that you remember the key concepts of the course. If there are things that you can't remember, then build them into your study programme to go over again. This ensures there are no gaps in your learning.

Your notes should be condensed to include all the key points – especially those that you have most difficulty remembering. Write any really hard-to-remember key points in the spaces at the top or bottom of the pages so they will stand out when you flick through them. Look over these notes **every day** from about **two weeks** before the exam, so the points become really familiar and you remember them easily.

If there is something you still find difficult to remember on the day before the exam, write the key points onto a large sheet of paper, hang this on your bedroom wall and look at it frequently until you feel you have got the information in your memory.

CONTINUOUS ASSESSMENT

At National 4 level, your work is submitted to your teachers and marked in school. Your grade is based on this work, so you must always meet the deadlines for drafts and final submissions. Your teacher will set aside time to mark the work of the class and their marking schedule might not allow any time for late submissions.

In some subjects, project and practical work undertaken throughout the year contributes to your final mark. Think of this as a way of getting marks in the bank before you even enter the exam room. Always ask for your teacher's or tutor's guidance when you are doing these pieces of work.

Whatever piece of work you are doing, make sure that you incorporate your teacher's advice, along with the techniques you have learned in this book. The BrightRED Study Guides are written to support these assessments, and many have dedicated sections for assignments and portfolios.

THINGS TO DO AND THINK ABOUT

Practise using the higher order thinking questions in your continuous assessments.

BEFORE THE EXAM 1

You need to go into externally marked exams with a good idea of what to expect. You obviously won't know the exact questions, but you should know the format of the exam (whether it involves multiple choice questions, short or longer answers). You should also know how to **answer** different types of questions, depending on the words used to **ask** the questions.

UNDERSTANDING THE QUESTIONS

It is crucial that you can interpret from the wording of the question **how** the examiners want you to answer it and **what** specific information they are looking for.

An obvious first hint is how many marks are to be awarded for the answer. This will give you an indication of how much information to include. An answer that awards six marks will expect a lot more depth and detail than an answer that awards two marks.

Next, look at the words used to find out what information the examiners are looking for. Questions often contain one of the following four **instruction words**:

- Describe
- Explain
- Discuss
- Justify

We're going to look at each of these instruction words in more detail, because each one requires a different type of approach to answering exam questions.

DESCRIBE QUESTIONS

Describe questions usually ask about processes or events. Give a solid, concise start to your answer by using the definitions you have for the keywords.

Detail the process or event step by step, and in the correct order to give flow to the answer. The examiner should be able to build an understanding from reading your answer.

Questions that ask you to **describe in detail** usually carry more marks and so require a longer, more in-depth answer. Select the appropriate information in your memory that relates to your keywords to add depth and detail for higher mark answers.

DON'T FORGET

Do not assume the examiner knows what you mean – you have to write each step.

EXAMPLE

Question 11— Environmental hazards

(a) Study Diagram Q11.

Use the information in Diagram Q11 to describe, in detail, where tropical storms are found throughout the world.

(4 marks)

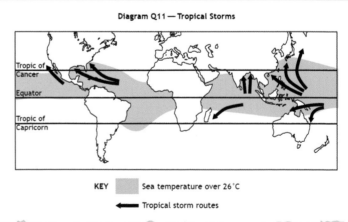

Diagram Q11 — Tropical Storms

KEY — Sea temperature over 26°C — Tropical storm routes

TIPS ON HOW TO ANSWER A 'DESCRIBE' QUESTION

This is a **describe in detail** question. You are expected to apply your knowledge in context, so will need to know the names of the areas, include the impact of sea temperature and the directions of the winds. You will also need to apply your higher order thinking skills here.

The information you need to answer this question is found in the extract from the *BrightRED Study Guide N5 Geography* below. Look for the keywords. **Cyclones** and **Typhoons** are already highlighted for you so the information in these sentences is really important. Diagram 11 also has the sea temperature on it, so find and use references to this.

LOCATION OF TROPICAL STORMS

Severe tropical storms are known as hurricanes in the North Atlantic and Caribbean. They are called **cyclones** in the Indian Ocean and **typhoons** in the Pacific Ocean and South China Sea. It is rare for tropical storms to form in the southern Atlantic or Pacific. These storms normally move or track in a westerly direction but can sometimes become stationary or stalled for many hours, inflicting sustained damage on areas unlucky enough to be affected. As storms **dissipate** or die out, they may move north-easterly in the northern hemisphere and south-easterly in the southern hemisphere. As they move away from tropical and sub-tropical regions, there is no longer enough warm surface water to drive them so they become less intense. However, storms which were originally Atlantic hurricanes do sometimes track all the way across the Atlantic, arriving on the shores of northern Europe to cause considerable disruption.

Questions 1 and 2(a) in the 'Things to do and think about' extract below will also help you to think of the information you need to answer this question.

THINGS TO DO AND THINK ABOUT

1 Study the map showing the locations of tropical storms. Give the names (using an atlas if necessary) of at least six countries affected by:
   (a) hurricanes in the North Atlantic and Caribbean
   (b) typhoons in the Pacific and South China Sea

2 Copy and complete these statements. Choose from the answers listed below.

storm surge	50 kilometres	1000 kilometres
252 km/h	27°C	119 km/h
typhoon	eye	

   (a) In a tropical storm, sea surface temperature has to be at least ...
   (b) The centre of a tropical storm is called the ...
   (c) Sea level rise caused by tropical storms is called a ...
   (d) A severe tropical storm in south-east Asia is called a ...
   (e) A tropical storm becomes a hurricane when wind speeds reach ...
   (f) A category 5 hurricane has wind speeds over ...
   (g) The diameter of a tropical storm can be over ...
   (h) The width of the calm area at the eye of the storm can be up to ...

3 Explain how a tropical storm forms.

THINGS TO DO AND THINK ABOUT

In the next section, we will look at explain questions.

BEFORE THE EXAM 2

EXPLAIN QUESTIONS

Explain questions usually ask for a description with reasons. Sometimes the word 'explain' will be omitted and you will just be asked to 'give reasons'.

EXAMPLE

Question 8 — Population Pyramids for Kenya and the United States

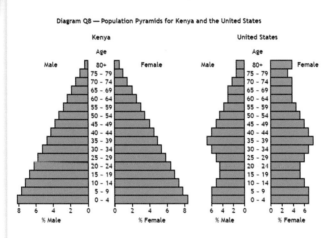

Diagram Q8 — Population Pyramids for Kenya and the United States

Look at Diagram Q8.

Explain the differences between the population structures of Kenya and the United States. **(6 marks)**

TIPS ON HOW TO ANSWER AN 'EXPLAIN' QUESTION

This question might seem daunting if you don't know much about the populations of Kenya or the United States. However, you are being asked to process the information you have been given using the principles of **apply**, **analyse** and **evaluate**, which you have practised many times across your subjects.

The following extract from the *Bright Red Study Guide N5 Geography* contains information on dependency ratio and a comparison of developed and developing countries that will help you to answer this question.

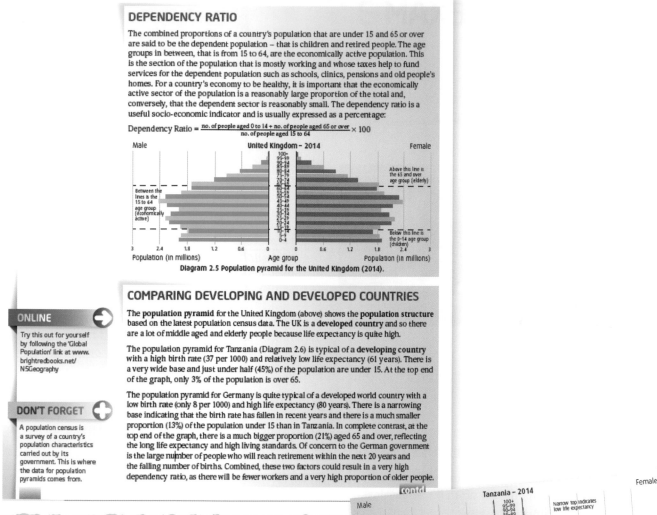

DEPENDENCY RATIO

The combined proportions of a country's population that are under 15 and 65 or over are said to be the dependent population – that is children and retired people. The age groups in between, that is from 15 to 64, are the economically active population. This is the section of the population that is mostly working and whose taxes help to fund services for the dependent population such as schools, clinics, pensions and old people's homes. For a country's economy to be healthy, it is important that the economically active sector of the population is a reasonably large proportion of the total and, conversely, that the dependent sector is reasonably small. The dependency ratio is a useful socio-economic indicator and is usually expressed as a percentage:

$$\text{Dependency Ratio} = \frac{\text{no. of people aged 0 to 14} + \text{no. of people aged 65 or over}}{\text{no. of people aged 15 to 64}} \times 100$$

Diagram 2.5 Population pyramid for the United Kingdom (2014).

COMPARING DEVELOPING AND DEVELOPED COUNTRIES

The **population pyramid** for the United Kingdom (above) shows the **population structure** based on the latest population census data. The UK is a **developed country** and so there are a lot of middle aged and elderly people because life expectancy is quite high.

The population pyramid for Tanzania (Diagram 2.6) is typical of a **developing country** with a high birth rate (37 per 1000) and relatively low life expectancy (61 years). There is a very wide base and just under half (45%) of the population are under 15. At the top end of the graph, only 3% of the population is over 65.

The population pyramid for Germany is quite typical of a developed world country with a low birth rate (only 8 per 1000) and high life expectancy (80 years). There is a narrowing base indicating that the birth rate has fallen in recent years and there is a much smaller proportion (13%) of the population under 15 than in Tanzania. In complete contrast, at the top end of the graph, there is a much bigger proportion (21%) aged 65 and over, reflecting the long life expectancy and high living standards. Of concern to the German government is the large number of people who will reach retirement within the next 20 years and the falling number of births. Combined, these two factors could result in a very high dependency ratio, as there will be fewer workers and a very high proportion of older people.

contd

ONLINE

Try this out for yourself by following the 'Global Population' link at www.brightredbooks.net/N5Geography

DON'T FORGET

A population census is a survey of a country's population characteristics carried out by its government. This is where the data for population pyramids comes from.

Look for the keywords. The labels on the diagrams are particularly helpful and you should include them in your explanation. Remember, you might have to give brief descriptions. These will help to clarify your reasons.

You may be asked to explain **differences** or **similarities**. In this case, make sure you clearly show and give the reasons for the contrasts or differences between Kenya and the United States.

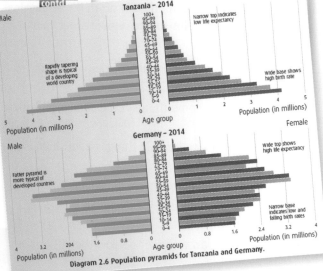

Diagram 2.6 Population pyramids for Tanzania and Germany.

THINGS TO DO AND THINK ABOUT

Use a past paper for one of your subjects to locate another 'explain' question. Refer to any class notes or study guides and use the techniques above to put together an answer.

BEFORE THE EXAM 3

DISCUSS QUESTIONS

Discuss questions ask you to present different points of view, or to review the possible variables.

EXAMPLE

Question 3

Discuss the effects of ICT on an organisation.

(5 marks)

TIPS ON HOW TO ANSWER A 'DISCUSS' QUESTION

In this question, you are asked for different points of view. 'Discuss' questions can often be the hardest to answer, and it helps to use higher order thinking questions such as:

- Why did that happen then but, not on another occasion?
- What caused some things to be similar and some different?
- Is there a link that made things seem similar or act the same way?
- Is there a historic, physical or emotional link?
- What are the reasons for things to be similar or different?
- What facts can you use to show the differences or similarities?
- Are these views facts or opinions? How reliable are they?

ICT can have both positive and negative effects on an organisation. To answer this example question, you would need to present a number of different key points:

ICT and robotic machinery can lead to increased productivity (✓) by producing more goods in less time. ICT can be expensive to install initially (✓), but can bring savings (✓) through increased productivity.

Some staff may be resistant to change (✓) and there may be training costs (✓) associated with the introduction of new systems. Some staff may be happier because teleworking will be possible, allowing staff to work at home (✓).

ICT can help to improve communications (✓) internally and externally. The organisation may gain a competitive edge (✓) over similar organisations who do not fully use ICT.

JUSTIFY QUESTIONS

Justify questions are looking for you to use evidence to support and explain your answer.

EXAMPLE

Question 1. (continued)

(b)   The circuit is now rearranged as shown below.

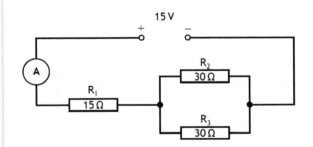

State how the reading on the ammeter compares to your answer in (a)(i).

Justify your answer by calculation.

(5 marks)

To help you answer 'justify' questions, ask yourself the higher order thinking questions such as:

- What evidence do I have?
- What did we use to show how this came about?
- Has someone developed a theory or published research showing a point of view?
- Can you use quotes to back up your point?
- Is there related information that affects or explains events?
- Are there any results of experiments that explain what has happened?

For this N5 Physics question, it is clear that the calculations from this circuit, and the one in (a) (i), provide the evidence for this answer.

In other subjects, you should use subject-specific vocabulary and examples to build up your evidence.

In English, quotes can provide the evidence to support your points.

In History, sometimes questions will ask you to 'evaluate' information from the source provided, as in the example below:

DON'T FORGET

Always show your working out in physics and maths, because this will be used to measure your understanding.

EXAMPLE

Source A

It is impossible to state exactly how much was given to the Duke of Atholl, the Marquis of Tweeddale and the Earls of Roxburghe, Marchmont and Cromartie without revealing exactly how much has been given to everybody else. So far, this has been kept a secret and revealing this information at present would cause embarrassment.

Evaluate the usefulness of Source A as evidence of why some Scots were persuaded to support the Act of Union. (You may want to comment on who wrote it, when they wrote it, why they wrote it, what they say or what has been missed out.)   (5 marks)

If the question has (like the one above) suggested things for you to focus on – such as who, when, why and so on – you can use this to help you structure your answer. Once you complete your answer, go back to the question and check that you have included all the suggested points.

THINGS TO DO AND THINK ABOUT

Select an answer that you have completed from a past paper. Look at the question and underline the instruction word. Now underline the parts of your answer that relate to the instruction word. If you have more than one instruction word, use a different colour to underline for each.

To develop the skill of applying the instruction words, practise using them. Keep referring back to the examples to check that you are using the correct type of words and phrases. Build up your own bank of phrases.

BEFORE THE EXAM 4

KEY CONCEPTS AND KEY FEATURES

Imagine you are the examiner. Long before the national qualifications are sat, there will have been many meetings between examiners and markers to identify the specific areas of the course work to be tested and the marks to be awarded for these identified areas. These are called key concepts or topics and are sub-divided into key features or sub-sections. You might already have identified these and be using them as the main strands and branches of your mind maps.

If you do not know the key concepts or key features in your course work, ask your teacher or tutor to tell you what they are or check them on the SQA website. Some of the study guides use the key concepts as the chapter headings with the key features as sub-headings.

Knowing the key concepts and key features can help you to:

- structure your revision to ensure that you cover all relevant areas
- understand which area of knowledge the question is expecting you to answer
- respond quickly and effectively to the exam questions as your brain recalls keywords and the related bank of knowledge for that topic
- have confidence in your exam answers
- achieve success in the exams.

ACTIVITY

Take an area of your work and break it down by identifying the key concepts and key features. If you have difficulty identifying these, it could mean that you don't fully understand the topic and so you won't be able to identify what information the question is seeking. Don't be afraid to ask your teacher or tutor to help you with this task.

SUBJECT-SPECIFIC VOCABULARY

Subjects tend to have words or phrases specific to their key concepts and key features. During your reflective thinking and when studying and preparing for your exams make sure that you:

- learn the correct subject-specific terminology and use it in your answers (use your preferred learning styles to do this)
- give a brief definition of the term or word. Knowing the definitions will be a great help when a question asks you to **describe** or **explain** the term.

The reflective thinking process – identifying keywords, adding definitions and applying them – will help your brain to get into the habit of identifying, using and applying subject-specific vocabulary.

It can help to make up a dictionary of keywords as part of your study notes. Use the **look/cover/write/check** method to learn these off by heart. Study books and guides can sometimes let you know exactly which words to use.

PAST PAPERS

Once you have completed all, or key parts, of the course, look over past exam papers and practise writing your own answers. This is a recognised and effective method of improving exam performance. Compare your answers with good or 'model' answers. This will allow you to assess what you did well and what you still need to improve upon.

When you analyse or mark your answers, highlight the areas you did well in with a colour coding or with a tick or comment (see pages 50–53). This is important because it lets you see that you have learned that area well, and will only need to look over this at intervals prior to your exam.

Highlight the areas that need more work and build them into your study plan. When you next complete a past paper question, check that you have done better and flag this up accordingly.

After you have answered a few questions, you will probably find that you're able to predict the sorts of things you are asked in an exam. This means you are starting to **apply** the higher order thinking questions yourself. Remember to use this in your study and reflective thinking.

DON'T FORGET

Don't always choose the questions you find easy. Try answering the one you think you might panic over if it came up in the exam. This way you will push yourself, learn more and will be prepared for every eventuality.

EXAM TIMINGS

As you get closer to the exam, start to develop an awareness of how long it should take you to answer the paper – without your study notes. Once you have a good knowledge of the content, time yourself while you are answering past paper questions.

Each subject and each paper will be slightly different. Some might be divided into three or four equal sections. If this is the case, work out how long you should spend on each section. At the top of your question paper write down a time plan, so you know when you have to change to the next question. Say, for example, that the exam starts at 9:00am, is one-hour long and is split into four sections. Your time plan would look like this:

Section 1 – 9:00am

Section 2 – 9:15am

Section 3 – 9:30am

Section 4 – 9:45am

If the paper doesn't divide up easily into sections, then simply work out what half-time is and try to get halfway through the paper by that time. For example, if a paper is an hour long, begins at 9:00am and has 14 questions all with the same number of marks, you should aim to finish question 7 by 9.30am.

Remember to allow time to read through the paper. The format and number of questions will vary from subject to subject, so practise doing as many past papers as you can to familiarise yourself with the questions and how long they take.

Stick to your time plan as much as possible. If you spend extra time on one section, it might get you one or two additional marks by adding more depth and detail, but it will reduce the amount of time you have for other questions, and if you don't have enough time to answer them all, you could lose more marks overall than you gained.

This is a skill you should practise against the clock. It also gets you used to the time pressure of the exam. When practising at home, use an alarm clock or set the alarm on your mobile phone to help you pace your answers.

THINGS TO DO AND THINK ABOUT

Imagine you are making up an exam question.

1. Write the question. Start off with a fairly straightforward question using only one instruction, such as **describe**.

2. List, in bullet points, the key concepts and features for which marks would be awarded.

3. Practise answering the question.

4. Swap questions with a study buddy and carry out steps 2 and 3. Discuss your thoughts with them.

5. Repeat steps 1–4, but this time make the question more complicated by including two instructions such as **describe and explain** or **describe and discuss**.

ANSWER PLANS 1

For essay-type answers, plan what you are going to write **before** you write it. Before you make a start on the plan, you need to:

- identify the key concept or features that the question is asking about
- decide on the style of your answer from the instruction words in the question.

THE IMPORTANCE OF PLANNING

Planning will help you to:

- structure your answer, giving it an organised, logical flow
- ensure that you include all the key features and points
- develop discussion points
- stick to your time plan.

The plan is a brief note of your initial thoughts. It should be no more than a few lines and will contain the main bullet points, key words or phrases that will form the basis of your answer. You could draw arrows or number the main points to get a good order and flow to your answer.

As you are writing your answer, jot down any good ideas that come into your mind before you forget them, then continue writing your answer. When you have finished writing, go back and decide where to put them in your answer. Remember, the plan should be made of brief notes – it's not a long piece of writing.

Visual learners might find it easier to draw a brief mind-map or spider diagram.

Let's look at the question below, and at the example of an **answer plan** that you could develop to help you answer it.

EXAMPLE

Explain why you would be a good candidate for a sales job.

In this example, the four key points were identified first, and additional thoughts and ideas came later. Each of these points could now generate at least a paragraph in the response.

1. Personal qualities – good with people
   good listener
   enthusiastic – inspire

2. Experience – part-time job   career plan – sales
   reference   work experience

3. Product knowledge – easy to learn about product

4. Interests – would commit the time – well organised

ACTIVITY

Choose your favourite book, film or song. Draw up a brief plan to explain why you like it so much. Categorise each key issue separately as in the example on the previous page. You could refer to the storyline, characters, how you relate to it, and so on.

Practise drawing up plans in the months before your exams. Not all subjects and exams need extended answers, so look at past papers to see when plans would be helpful.

Auditory learners might prefer to develop plans in their head rather than on paper. If it works for you, then that is perfectly OK. However, if a new idea pops into your head while you are writing your answer, it is still a good idea to jot down keywords or prompts to ensure that you remember to include it in your answer. You could do this by making a note in the margin or at the top or bottom of the page.

THINGS TO DO AND THINK ABOUT

For longer answers, do brief plans for both your stronger and your weaker subjects. The framework will help your brain to draw on the appropriate knowledge to make your answer flow.

DON'T FORGET

Cross out your plan so the examiner knows that it's not to be marked with the rest of the answer.

ANSWER PLANS 2

PRESENTATION AND LAYOUT

Your answer plan should help you to identify the key points in your answer, and the order they should go in. This puts the points into a logical order and gives flow to your answer, making it easier for the examiner to read.

- Try to **write neatly** but don't spend too much time trying to make it really neat and then find that you don't have enough time to finish.
- Learn the **diagrams** and **graphs** that are in your notes. A well-labelled diagram can save you a lot of time as you won't need to write a lengthy description.
- Split your work into **paragraphs** and leave a **space** between them. The space makes it easier to read, and if you realise that you've missed something out you can always insert it into the space.
- **Number** your answers clearly so that there can be no doubt which question you are answering when the examiner marks it.

Most people – especially those who find reading difficult – find it easier to read passages that have spaces between each key point or paragraph. This is a technique you should use in your notes as well as in your exam answers.

ACTIVITY

Read the following passage and compare it with the text in the **'presentation and layout'** section above.

> From your rough plan for your answer you will now have the key points and the order they should go in. This puts the points into a logical order and gives flow to your answer, making it easier for the examiner to read. Try to write in neat handwriting but don't spend too much time trying to make it really neat and then find that you don't have enough time to finish. Learn the diagrams and graphs which are in your notes. A well-labelled diagram can save you a lot of time as you won't need to write a lengthy description. Split your work into paragraphs and leave a space between them. The space makes it easier to read and if you realise that you've missed something out you can always insert it into the space. Number your answers clearly so that there can be no doubt which question you are answering when the examiner marks it.

DON'T FORGET

Bullet points and highlighting (as used in the 'presentation and layout' passage) also help to identify the key points.

Which passage did you find easier to read (tick the one which most applies):

- the 'presentation and layout' passage with spaces between the paragraphs and underlining
- or the 'activity' passage with no spaces?

EFFECTIVE WRITING

Write in concise sentences – don't waffle. Having identified the key points you want to make, use subject-specific vocabulary. This can cut down the number of words you have to write. Here's an example:

EXAMPLE

Use subject-specific vocabulary.

instead of

Use the particular words which are used in the subject to accurately identify processes or procedures.

Check that you are using the key point only once. Repeating the same thing can waste valuable time in an exam if you have already been awarded the mark. You won't be awarded another mark for the same piece of information. Focus on working through your answer plan.

Writing effectively is a skill that you can develop with practice. Look at sample good answers to see how useful, accurate key phrases can reduce the amount you need to write. This will help you to answer more quickly. It will also make your answers clearer and more concise, and will cut out unnecessary repetition and waffle. Use the marking instructions from the SQA past papers as they often contain key phrases that you can learn.

You can also save time in an exam by incorporating a diagram in your writing and referring to its labels. It gives your answer a structure and you can use it as a checklist to ensure that you have included all the key points.

Make a list of good phrases, definitions and words and learn them using your preferred learning styles. Create a special vocabulary page for each subject on paper, as a poster or as a Word document on your computer. You should now be able to use them in your own answers. Once you have developed this skill, make up your own concise phrases and sentences. You should notice the improvement it makes to both your writing process and your finished work. It will also improve your confidence in exams.

DON'T FORGET

Use the good phrases you highlighted when you colour-coded your work.

THINGS TO DO AND THINK ABOUT

Write an answer to a question that you know has a sample answer. (If you can't find one, ask your teacher to source one for you.) Compare your answer to the sample answer and underline or highlight the key points in each.

Now highlight the best, most concise phrases in each answer. If your answer has a lot of highlighted phrases, then you've done a good job. If there are a lot more phrases highlighted on the sample answer, then this is an area you obviously need to work on.

IN THE EXAM

You have worked really hard during the build-up to the exam, so now it's time to put everything you have learned in this study guide into practice. Do this, and you can be confident that you will perform well.

The following **exam checklist** can help you to gain marks in the exam. Make this part of your routine when you are practising past paper questions.

THE EXAM CHECKLIST

1. READ THE INSTRUCTIONS CAREFULLY

Read the instructions carefully to find out exactly how much time you have and how many questions you have to answer in that time. (Don't answer 12 questions when you are only asked to answer three.)

2. READ THE WHOLE QUESTION FIRST

Read the whole question through before you begin to answer it, or you might miss something vital. Doing this will also give you an overview of what is required, so you can begin to plan your answer. Your plan should include:

- key points
- order of points.

Make sure you know exactly what the question is asking!

3. NOTE HOW MANY MARKS ARE TO BE AWARDED

The example below gives you an indication of the expected length of the answer – the more marks, the more depth and detail required in the answer.

> **EXAMPLE**
>
> (a)   Select an aspect of fitness. Describe how you assessed this aspect of fitness both within and outwith your chosen activity.
> (6 marks)

4. WHICH INSTRUCTION WORDS ARE USED?

The two parts of the following question use different instructions – describe and discuss. The information you include in your answer should depend on the instruction words used (see pages 74–79).

> **EXAMPLE**
>
> (b)   Describe your performance in comparison to a quality performance in your chosen activity.
> (6 marks)

> (c)   Discuss a training programme you followed that took into account your strengths and any development needs you may have.
> (6 marks)

5. UNDERLINE THE KEYWORDS IN THE QUESTION

When you <u>underline</u> the keywords, don't forget to include the instruction words. Refer back to the question from time to time to make sure that you are fully answering the question and haven't gone off track.

6. ANSWER YOUR STRONGEST SECTION FIRST

Begin with the question you feel most confident about answering. If you write a good answer, it will give you a psychological lift and help you to tackle questions that you feel less confident about.

7. WRITE THE TIMES

Write the time that you should start each new question at the top of the question paper (if appropriate). This will help you to schedule your answers and keep on track so that you manage to complete the paper in the time allowed.

8. USE DIAGRAMS

Use diagrams and graphs. They can help you understand the question (especially in the sciences). Diagrams and graphs can contain a lot of very concise and detailed information, and will also let your examiner see that you know and understand the topic.

This simple diagram demonstrates that you know what the lungs look like and what the different parts are called. Drawing and labelling a diagram is much more effective than trying to write a description.

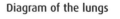

Diagram of the lungs

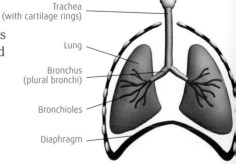

Trachea (with cartilage rings)

Lung

Bronchus (plural bronchi)

Bronchioles

Diaphragm

DON'T FORGET

Diagrams and graphs are not works of art – do not spend a lot of time on them, but make sure they are clear and that any labels are legible. Good diagrams can save you time.

9. IF YOU ARE RUNNING OUT OF TIME – PRIORITISE

If you find yourself short of time near the end of the exam, you will need to judge whether you would be best staying on the same question or if you could possibly get more marks by writing out the basics for another question. Look for questions that you know are easier to get marks for.

10. IF YOU ARE RUNNING OUT OF TIME – USE BULLET POINTS

Claw back some time by using bulleted lists instead of formal sentences. Make sure you link the bullet points into your answer. Example 1 shows the use of bullet points while Example 2 contains the same information written out fully.

EXAMPLE

To save time in an exam:
- *use bullet points*
- *use diagrams – labelled*
- *note the main points*
- *link them into the answer*

EXAMPLE

If you are struggling to complete the exam paper in the given time, then look to use shortcuts. These could include using bullet points rather than writing points into longer sentences. Use diagrams which may save time by not writing long, detailed explanations. Of course, label the diagrams so they show how they backed up the answer. Attempt to include the main points for which marks would be awarded. Finally, ensure that you have linked the bullet points into the answer so it meets the requirements of the question.

11. IF YOU HAVE TIME LEFT AT THE END OF THE EXAM

If you have time left at the end of the exam, use it to do the following:

- Go back to any sections that you missed out or feel you didn't answer as well as you could. Try to complete the answer or add more depth and detail into your work.

- Read over your answers. Make sure that what you have written is what you meant and will be understood by the examiner. You can also correct any spelling or grammatical errors.

- If you find you have made a mistake, correct it by using the space in the margin if necessary. If you don't have space, then draw a line through the incorrect part and put the amendment at the end of the answer paper. Write a comment to tell the examiner to look for the correct answer at the end of the paper – for example:

> Please note: 2b is continued at the end of the answer paper.

- At the end of the paper, clearly mark which question the amendment is for – for example:

> Question 2b continued.

DON'T FORGET

Listen carefully to the instructions the invigilator gives you at the start of the exam in case there are any changes or errors in the paper.

THINGS TO DO AND THINK ABOUT

As you go into the exam room, your adrenalin will probably be pumping and you will feel nervous. That's natural. Take a deep breath, start to read the paper and focus on the techniques and knowledge you have used in your preparation to give you the confidence to produce great answers.

After the exams, sit back, relax and look forward to your results – you've worked for them!

DEVELOPING LIFELONG SKILLS

The learning and reflective thinking skills you have developed have aimed to help you to perform well in all types of assessments. However, that is not their only application. You can continue to develop and adapt these skills to help you deal with new challenges throughout your working life.

As our society evolves and changes over time, so will our work and personal and social lives. Working practices change with new knowledge and technology. For example, in the 1950s, scientists started to develop computers – large bulky equipment, unlike what we use today. In the late 1980s, commercial internet service providers began to trade. This revolutionised how businesses worked and how people communicated. By the middle of the 1990s, e-mail was in common use and the World Wide Web (www) made social networking, blogs, forums and online shopping possible, causing huge commercial and cultural changes in our society. Can you imagine being without the internet or your mobile phone?

ACTIVE LEARNING

As an active learner you are involved in and have control over your learning. Education Scotland defined active learning as 'learning which engages and challenges children's thinking using real-life and imaginary situations.' (2010).

Now that you have developed these skills, you will use them in 'real-life and imaginary situations' as you move from school to college, work or university to learn new things and plan for the future. This is called **lifelong learning**.

THE RED ARROW LEARNING TRIANGLE

Throughout life you remain the most important aspect of this triangle. Your ability to gather information from colleagues, educators and your own search for knowledge puts you in control of the direction of your career. This will allow you to use your preferred learning and thinking styles and you will feel more comfortable, confident and happier working in your areas of strength, allowing you to perform at a higher level.

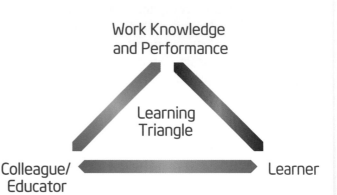

LIFELONG LEARNING

If you possess the skills for lifelong learning, you will feel comfortable and able to cope with social and work-related changes. Knowing that you have the skills to confidently adapt and meet the demands and challenges of new situations, reduces stress levels and leads to a happier lifestyle. It is really important to have a good work-life balance. If you get too stressed about changes and developments at work, then it can impact on your mood and affect how you interact with your family and friends.

The higher order thinking skills will help you to consider and come up with solutions. The thinking questions will use your growing knowledge and experiences so your brain can make the connections to allow you to make informed decisions or predictions.

REFLECTIVE THINKING

During reflective thinking, your brain uses keywords and definitions to access banks of knowledge and uses the higher order thinking questions to apply, analyse, evaluate and create solutions and outcomes.

Because you have used this process continually during your school learning, you will begin to do it automatically, without thinking about it. You will, therefore, be able to quickly adapt your skills to meet the demands of, for example, a new job, college or university.

MENTAL REHEARSAL

Mental rehearsal builds on reflective thinking. Once you come up with a solution through reflective thinking, going over it or 'rehearsing' in your mind lets you:

- check things over to ensure that what you are planning actually works. This may be easier for the more logical left brain thinkers but will help the creative right brain thinkers check that they have all the relevant stages covered.
- go over something again and again in your mind, strengthening the brain connections and helping the brain to recall information quickly and accurately.
- think through different options to work out which may be best or to prepare for a situation you are unsure of.

As you mentally rehearse and go over things in your mind, you are practising that scenario or, in other words, you are taking it through the associative stage of development. If the scenario changes, then you will be able to react autonomously, adapting your response to meet the new demands or conditions.

Kinaesthetic learners can be particularly good at mental rehearsal as the brain is doing all the work apart from physically applying it.

USING THINKING SKILLS IN THE POST-SCHOOL TRANSITION

It is probably easier to use these skills in college and university as they are similar learning environments, but there are some basic **employability** and enterprise skills that should be applied in all contexts.

FIRST IMPRESSIONS

You only get one chance at this and if you get it wrong you might have to put a lot of effort into changing someone's view of you. When someone first meets you, their 'system 1', subconscious brain will start to make decisions about you based on what they see and hear. These thoughts might be very wrong, but once they have formed them it takes effort to change that view.

Think through the context and evaluate how you should present yourself. For example, turning up to an interview for an office job in a tracksuit, or dressing for a night out when you report for work on a construction site, would not create a good first impression.

Think about how you want other people to 'see' you.

TIMEKEEPING

Regularly turning up late for work can result in losing your job and you will miss vital course work at college or university. Having a reputation for being late is a bad thing, and can have a negative effect on your performance and how other people view you. It could affect your promotion chances.

If you are travelling at busy times, remember to give yourself more time.

COMMUNICATE

Don't wait to be told to do things and ask if you are unsure. If you finish a task, check you have done it well and then go and seek out your next task. If you are unsure about something or need clarification, ask someone for help rather than do something wrong or even have, or cause, an accident.

EVALUATION

Reflect on what you are about to do and check it is safe and appropriate. Remember that sometimes instructions and directions get confused or are misunderstood. If you're not sure about something, ask for clarification.

If you are aware of things that could be improved, suggest how this can be done to your line manager or supervisor. If it is a health and safety issue you are unsure or concerned about, always bring it to someone's attention.

INITIATIVE

This is using your higher order thinking skills in context. Ask the questions:

- **Remember**: What is ...? What happened after ...?
- **Understand**: How would you explain ...? Tell in your own words ...
- **Apply**: How would you solve ...? What can you use to explain ...?
- **Analyse**: What is similar or different to ...? Is the information based on fact or opinion?
- **Evaluate**: What shows that ...? What evidence supports your view?
- **Create**: How could you improve/develop ...? What might be a solution to ...?

It's good to know that you have the initiative to identify a task that needs to be done and the skills to do it.

THINGS TO DO AND THINK ABOUT

Learn to learn – and develop skills for education and beyond!

APPENDIX 1 – INSTRUCTIONS

INSTRUCTIONS FOR MEMORY GAME 1A

1. Ask the player to look at the pictures on sheet A (page 91) for one minute exactly. You should time them, telling them when to start and finish.

2. Cover up the pictures and ask them to write down what they saw. Don't let them look at the pictures again.

3. The answers are:
   trousers, spade, chair, TV, glasses, banana, ship, clock, books, phone, hammer, motorbike, spoon, rollerblade and hairbrush.

4. Give one point for every correct answer. Count up the points for a mark out of 15.

INSTRUCTIONS FOR MEMORY GAME 1B

1. Ask the player to look at the pictures on sheet B (page 92) for one minute exactly. You should time them, telling them when to start and finish.

2. Cover up the pictures and ask them to write down which pictures were **not** on sheet A. Don't let them look at the pictures again.

3. The answers are:
   apple, watch, camera and fork.

4. Give one point for every correct answer. Count up the points for a mark out of 4.

INSTRUCTIONS FOR MEMORY GAME 2A

1. Slowly and clearly, read out all the items in list 1 (page 93). When you have finished, read the list out again. Do not allow them to see the list.

2. Ask the player to write down everything they remember from the list. They should not write anything until the list has been read for the second time.

3. Once they have written all they can remember, read the list to them again so that they can mark off their correct answers (no marks deducted for incorrect answers). They should total their marks out of 14.

INSTRUCTIONS FOR MEMORY GAME 2B

1. Slowly and clearly, read out all the items in list 2 (page 93). When you have finished, read the list out again. Do not allow them to see the list.

2. Ask the player to write down everything they remember from the list. They should not write anything until the list has been read for the second time.

3. Once they have written all they can remember, read the list to them again so that they can mark off their correct answers (no marks deducted for incorrect answers). They should total their marks out of 14.

INSTRUCTIONS FOR MEMORY GAME 3

1. Ask the player to look at the list of television programmes (page 93) for one minute exactly. Nothing should be written down before the end of the minute.

2. At the end of the minute ask them to write down:
   • the day of the week the programmes are listed for
   • the channel number
   • each programme (1 mark for each programme).

3. Once they have written all they can remember read the list to them again so that they can mark off their correct answers (no marks deducted for incorrect answers). They should total their marks out of 11.

INSTRUCTIONS FOR MEMORY GAME 4

1. Slowly and clearly, read out the football results (page 93). When you have finished, read the list out again. Do not allow the player to see the list.

2. After you have read out the list twice, ask them to write the answers to these questions:
   • Who did Hearts play?
   • Which team scored the highest number of goals?
   • How many did they score?
   • How many draws were there?
   • What was the Airdie vs Ross County score?
   • How many goals were there in the Hibs vs Aberdeen game?

3. Once they have answered all the questions, read the list to them again so that they can mark off their correct answers (no marks deducted for incorrect answers). They should total their marks out of 6.

MEMORY GAME 1A SHEET A

MEMORY GAME 2A

List 1
Apple
Box
Cap
Dog
Egg
Foot
Grass
Hotel
iPod
Jacket
Key
Liquorice
Money
Newspaper

MEMORY GAME 2A

List 2
Hair
Horse
Handcuff
Hutch
Hose
Helmet
Hammer
Home
Hen
Hut
Hat
Honey
Harp
Head

MEMORY GAME 3

Channel 321
Thursday

4:35pm	Scooby-Doo
5:00pm	Newsround
5:15pm	Pointless
6:00pm	National news
6:30pm	Local news and weather
7:00pm	Emmerdale
7:30pm	Coronation Street
8:00pm	Pets – Wild at Heart
8:30pm	Location, Location, Location

MEMORY GAME 4

Raith Rovers	3	Kilmarnock	2
Rangers	2	Celtic	2
Hearts	1	Falkirk	0
Airdrie United	0	Ross County	0
Queens Park	0	St. Mirren	3
Arbroath	1	Dundee United	2
Hibernian	4	Aberdeen	5
Albion	1	Dunfermline Athletic	6

Now read out the following questions:

1. Who did Hearts play?
2. Which team scored the highest number of goals?
3. How many did they score?
4. How many draws were there?
5. What was the Airdrie vs Ross County score?
6. How many goals were there in the Hibs vs Aberdeen game?

The answers are:

1. Falkirk
2. Dunfermline
3. six
4. two
5. nil – nil
6. nine

APPENDIX 2 – CURRICULUM FOR EXCELLENCE: THE FOUR CAPACITIES

Successful learners

with:
- enthusiasm and motivation for learning
- determination to reach high standards of achievement
- openness to new thinking and ideas

and able to:
- use literacy, communication and numeracy skills
- use technology for learning
- think creatively and independently
- learn independently and as part of a group
- make reasoned evaluations
- link and apply different kinds of learning in new situations

Confident individuals

with:
- self-respect
- a sense of physical, mental and emotional well being
- secure values and beliefs
- ambition

and able to:
- relate to others and manage themselves
- pursue a healthy and active lifestyle
- be self-aware
- develop and communicate their own beliefs and view of the world
- live as independently as they can
- assess risk and make informed decisions
- achieve success in different areas of activity

Responsible citizens

with:
- respect for others
- commitment to participate responsibly in political, economic, social and cultural life

and able to:
- develop knowledge and understanding of the world and Scotland's place in it
- understand different beliefs and cultures
- make informed choices and decisions
- evaluate environmental, scientific and technological issues
- develop informed, ethical views of complex issues

Curriculum for Excellence's Four Capacities

Effective contributors

with:
- an enterprising attitude
- resilience
- self-reliance

and able to:
- communicate in different ways and in different settings
- work in partnership and in teams
- take the initiative and lead
- apply critical thinking in new contexts
- create and develop
- solve problems

10 GLOSSARY

3Rs – the three-stage learning/study process of **review, remember, recall**.

Abbreviations and symbols – used to shorten or code information to make it easier to learn and remember.

Active learning – where activities and processes that fully engage and stimulate the brain lead to more effective learning.

Answer plans – method for setting out and structuring an answer.

Associative – the second stage of skill development (the practice stage).

Auditory thinker/learner – thinks and/or learns mainly through hearing or talking.

Autonomous – the third stage of skill development (the automatic stage).

Bloom's Revised Taxonomy – hierarchy of thinking skills developed by Bloom and adapted by Anderson & Krathwohl, 2001.

Brain computer – term used to indicate that the brain is working to process information.

Chunking – the breaking down of material to be learned into smaller parts to make it easier to process and remember.

Cognitive – the first stage of skill acquisition (the learning stage).

Colour coding – where different colours are used to highlight aspects of work such as strengths or keywords. This helps in self-evaluating work when improving or re-drafting.

Colour/symbol method – where different colours and a range of symbols are used to evaluate and highlight the strengths and weaknesses in a piece of work.

Confident individuals – enjoy and value successful study as one of the tools to help achieve learning and career targets.

Correcting work – where work is evaluated by confirming strong points and strengthening weak points.

Curriculum for Excellence – Scottish Education's revised system. This promotes a coherent, enriched, flexible curriculum, which ensures that every pupil has the opportunity to achieve the knowledge, skills and attributes for learning, life and work.

Cycle of learning – the complete process of learning from identifying current learning habits to using the 3Rs.

Definition – the meaning of a word or phrase.

Describe – detail the process or event step by step.

Diagrams and graphs – if these are included in notes made during the review stage, they make it easier to commit information to memory in the remember stage and can be included in answers in the recall stage.

Discuss – explain and apply different points of view.

Effective contributors – are active and valued participants in the learning process.

Employability skills – transferrable skills that are necessary for all jobs.

Exam checklist – a list of things to be aware of during an exam.

Exam timings – a plan that shows the amount of time you need to spend on each question/section of an exam to complete the exam within the time limits.

Explain – give a description with reasons.

Health and wellbeing – this is an integral part of Curriculum for Excellence and is concerned with the social, physical, mental and emotional wellbeing of every pupil.

Higher order thinking skills – the skills of applying, analysing, evaluating and creating as outlined in Bloom's Revised Taxonomy.

Higher order thinking questions – specific questions used to apply higher order thinking in context.

Ideal study hour – a time structure that applies review, remember and recall to maximise concentration, learning and the effectiveness of time spent on study.

Instruction words – the main asking words in exam questions: describe, explain, discuss, justify. These direct how the question should be answered.

Internet – Glow, BBC Bitesize, SQA, your school and many other websites provide interactive learning opportunities. These can be stimulating for visual, auditory and kinaesthetic learners.

Internet search – involves using the internet to research and access information. Care should be taken to ensure that the information is accurate. This can be done by cross-checking different, unrelated sources. The source of any information used should be acknowledged through referencing and bibliographies.

Justify – give evidence to explain/support your answer.

Key concepts – these are the key topic areas within each subject. SQA exam questions will be set on these concepts and they will be included in the markers' guidelines.

Key features – these are the key points of the key concepts and should be included in SQA exam responses.

Key points/words/phrases – these are integral to each stage of the 3Rs. They are identified during the review stage, learned in the remember stage and applied in context through the recall stage.

Kinaesthetic thinker/learner – thinks and/or learns mainly by doing.

Learning styles – a range of skills and techniques used to process and remember information. Each individual will have preferred styles that they are more comfortable with or find easier. A full range of learning styles should be practised to enable the learner to succeed in the wide range of learning activities experienced across the curriculum.

Literature search – involves looking through books, newspapers, journals and magazines for information.

Lifelong learning – learning that continues throughout life. This helps the learner to develop, adapt and grow within an evolving society.

Long-term memory – the ability to remember information over an extended period of time.

Look/cover/write/check – a crucial process to check whether information has been remembered. Can be adapted depending on the subject material being learned. Study supporters can make the process more enjoyable.

Memory prompts – these are cues such as mnemonics, diagrams and keywords that help the brain to recall a bank of information.

Mental rehearsal – this involves practising and visualising things in the mind.

Mind-maps – these are diagrams that use words, pictures and colour to show related information spreading out from a central theme. As the layout of the mind-map mimics the way the brain processes information, it is regarded as being a highly effective method of study for many people.

Mnemonics – these are used to remember lists or a number of points. The first letter of each word is used to form a new word or sentence (which can often be nonsensical). This word or sentence is then used as a memory prompt to help the brain remember a bank of information.

Organisational skills – this is a person's ability to create order and can range from organising study folders to keeping their bedroom tidy!

Paraphrase – putting somebody else's work into your own words.

Past papers – these are official SQA exam papers from previous years available online. Using past papers as part of a study programme helps with exam techniques.

Peer research – a group of pupils investigating and developing resources together in an organised manner.

Plagiarism – using someone's work without acknowledging who/where it came from.

Planning – planning essays and extended writing gives structure and flow to the work.

Preferred thinking/learning styles – every learner is unique and has specific ways of thinking and learning that they like best and probably use most. It is important to develop and use a wide range of styles to be able to meet the demands of the different learning activities.

Presentation and layout – setting out work clearly makes it easier to read. Using paragraphs, indentations, spaces and bullet points make key points stand out more and helps with the structure and flow of the work.

Quote – using someone's exact words by putting them into inverted commas ('...') and acknowledging where you got the quote from.

Recall – this is the final stage of the 3Rs. It involves using the information from the 'review' and 'remember' stages and the application of the higher level thinking skills: applying, analysing, evaluating and creativity.

Referencing and bibliography – this is the acknowledgement of all the materials consulted during research. Details of the authors and their materials will be mentioned in the bibliography.

Reflective thinking – the process that helps the brain to make connections between keywords, definitions and banks of knowledge and to apply the relevant information in a range of contexts. Used with higher order thinking skills.

Remember – the second stage of the 3Rs is committing information to memory, both short- and long-term. A range of methods should be used to support different types of learning and active learning.

Research – this involves using a range of resources, such as books and the internet, to find information on a chosen topic.

Responsible citizens – self-evaluate and make informed decisions that will help towards career aspirations.

Review – the first stage of the 3Rs in which information is condensed using keywords, mnemonics, diagrams, mind-maps and so on to form brief study notes.

Rhymes – this is a method to help the brain remember information.

Right/left brain – the right half of the brain processes information relating to creative, whole-picture activities while the left half of the brain processes logical, sequential thoughts. Most people are dominant in one half but the two sides link together.

Self-evaluation/assessment – involves analysing individual strengths and weaknesses. This is an essential process when improving work as it identifies the strong, mark-winning areas and highlights what can be improved upon.

Short-term memory – this is the ability of the brain to remember information for a few hours to a few days. The information needs to be revisited to start to move it to the long-term memory. Some information can be crammed into the short-term memory just before tests and will be forgotten fairly soon after the test.

SMARTER targets – these are goals which are: **s**pecific, **m**easureable, **a**chievable, **r**ealistic, **t**imescale, **e**valuated, **r**ecorded.

Spider diagram – this is a simplified form of a mind-map. Diagrams have a central theme with related ideas extending out from the centre.

Strengths – these are areas of success and could include, for example, making up good study notes in the 'review' stage, learning information thoroughly in the 'remember' stage and creatively applying these strengths with exam techniques in the 'recall' stage.

Structure – this is an outline to ensure that an essay flows and develops the key points in a related order.

Study buddies and study groups – these can be friends or school clubs. They support 3Rs learning by providing an opportunity to research, develop, learn and discuss material.

Study notes – these notes are a record of all the key information in a shortened, easy-to-read-and-use form. They are compiled during the 'review' stage, committed to memory during the 'remember' stage and act as prompts during the 'recall' stage to answer exam questions.

Study plan – this weekly or monthly diary records all key information for planning and doing study/homework. It includes personal and social commitments. It helps with organisational skills and also gives confidence when it shows how much study has been done.

Study programme – this progressively develops learning by applying the 3Rs study skills to meet longer-term learning targets.

Study skills – these are a range of techniques and tactics that are learned and practised. They should be developed and used throughout the 3Rs and matched to every individual's thinking and learning style to maximise learning potential and exam performance.

Study support – support from family and friends can make study more interesting and fun. It also lets them see how hard you are working.

Subject-specific vocabulary – these are words and phrases that are used in a particular context within a subject.

Successful learners – have learned, developed and practised a range of study skills that they have applied effectively through each of the 'review', 'remember' and 'recall' stages of the 3Rs.

Text language – shortened and abbreviated words can be used effectively to keep study notes short and easy to read. Text language should never be used in assessments.

Text maps – these are similar to mind-maps but contain words only (no pictures).

Thinking styles – these are the methods that the brain uses to take in and process information. The main methods used are auditory, visual and kinaesthetic but can also include taste, smell and touch. Most people will use a range of methods and these will vary according to the type of information being processed.

Visual thinker/learner – thinks/learns mainly by looking at information or seeing demonstrations.

Vocabulary – subjects often require specific words to be used. These words have clear subject-specific meanings and in some situations marks will be awarded for using the correct vocabulary appropriately.

Weaknesses – identifying and developing weaker skills or pieces of work is a key aspect of improving learning. There are a range of skills to support this, including the colour/symbol method.

Working memory – this is the short-term memory used in the cognitive stage of learning when doing classroom activities.